WALK TO
EMMAUS
THE UPPER ROOM®

chrysalis
THE UPPER ROOM®

JOURNEY
TO THE TABLE
THE UPPER ROOM®

FACE to FACE
THE UPPER ROOM®

EMMAUS MINISTRIES

COMMUNITY MANUAL

UPPER
ROOM BOOKS®
NASHVILLE

**For more information about The Walk to Emmaus
or to learn about other Emmaus Ministries resources**
see emmaus.upperroom.org/
or call the International Emmaus Ministries Office
at (877) 899-2780 ext.7113 or (615) 340-7113.

CONTENTS

Section 1—THE EMMAUS STORY   7

The Scripture Story   7
The Emmaus Ministries Family and The Upper Room   8
Introduction to Emmaus Ministries   12
Important Features of Emmaus Ministries Programs   13

Section 2—THE EMMAUS MINISTRIES COMMUNITY   19

Beginning an Emmaus Community   19
Beginning an Emmaus Ministry Program   21
Keeping Faith with the Emmaus Program Models   29
Beginning an International Emmaus Community   32
Community Board of Directors   32
Sample Bylaws and Board Structures   37

Section 3—LEADERSHIP   45

Boards and Committees   45
Team Selection   46
Team Formation and Experience   46
Community Gatherings and Training   46
Training Help from The Upper Room   48
Appendices   49
    Team Member Qualifications (Laity and Clergy)   49
    Clergy Qualifications   50
    Clergy Roles in Emmaus Ministries   51

Section 4—TEAMS   53

Team Leader Selection   53
Team Member Selection   55
Team Selection Responsibilities   56
Team Selection Guidelines   57
Team Formation   65

Section 5—SPONSORSHIP — 71

Sponsorship Training — 71
Chrysalis Parents' Meeting — 80
Sponsors' Hour — 82
A Model Sponsor — 82

Section 6—FOURTH DAY — 85

Fourth Day Members — 86
Fourth Day Follow-up Meeting — 86
Accountability Groups/Group Reunions — 89
Community Meetings or Gatherings — 98
Emmaus and Church Partnership — 104

Section 7—GENERAL REMINDERS — 109

Church Diversity — 109
Participants Leaving Before Completing the Event — 110
Leaning into the Fourth Day — 111
Keeping the Schedule — 112
Tone of Each Part of the Event and Team Disposition — 113
Distribution of Agape in Emmaus — 113
The Learning Process — 114
Honoring the Community-Building Process — 115
Baptism and the Emmaus Event — 115
Celebration of Holy Communion — 116
Being Slain in the Spirit and Other Phenomena — 116
"DeColores" in Emmaus Events — 117
Balancing Leadership of Chrysalis Events with Young People — 118
Parental Participation in Chrysalis — 118
Psychological Manipulation — 121
Sexual Harassment and Child Abuse Laws — 121

Section 8—SUGGESTED SUPPLIES — 123

Agape Room — 123
Registration — 124
Prayer Chapel — 124
Conference Room: General & Altar — 125
Conference Room: Tables & Participants — 126
Conference Room: Health & Beauty Aids — 127

Section 9—SAMPLE LETTERS AND HANDOUTS — 129

Registrar's Letter Acknowledging Receipt of Application — 129
Registrar's Acceptance Letter to Participant — 130
Registrar's Letter to Participant's Sponsor — 131
For Chrysalis: Registrar's Letter to Participant's Parents — 132

Sponsor's Letter to Request Agape Letters for Participant   133
Event Spiritual Director's Letter to Participant's Pastor   134
"Points to Remember" Handout for the Participant's Packet   135
"Things to Know" Handout for the Participant's Packet   136
Prayer Prompts for the Prayer Chapel   137

Section 10—RESOURCES   139

Emmaus Publications   139
Face to Face Resources   140
Other Resources   140

Section 11—EVENT BACKGROUND ROLE DESCRIPTIONS   141

Event Agape Coordinator   141
Event Facilities Coordinator   145
Event Kitchen Coordinator   148
Event Music/Entertainment Coordinator   152
Event Prayer Chapel Coordinator   153
Event Registrar   156
Event Sponsors' Hour Coordinator   158
Event Candlelight Service Coordinator   159
Event Supply/Literature Coordinator   160
Event Transportation/Housing Coordinator   161

SECTION 1— THE EMMAUS STORY

The following describes the basic intent and design of all Emmaus Ministries programs— Walk to Emmaus, Chrysalis, Face to Face, and Journey to the Table—while retelling the story of two disciples' experience with the risen Christ on the road to Emmaus. As you read this section you will discover the following:

- an overview of Emmaus Ministries;

- information about its relationship to The Upper Room®;

- a review of some important features, such as the strengths Emmaus Ministries brings to the church, the uniqueness of Emmaus Ministries among spiritual formation experiences, and a few aspects of Emmaus Ministries that may need explanation;

- an insight into the biblical, theological, psychological, and practical reasons behind some of the unique practices and dynamics of Emmaus Ministries programs.

Understanding the foundation of the programs will empower and motivate leaders and Communities, and give them the vision necessary to lead the programs faithfully.

THE SCRIPTURE STORY

The Gospel of Luke relates the story of the risen Christ appearing to two disciples who are walking along the road from Jerusalem to the town of Emmaus on the day of Resurrection. This experience depicts the heart and soul of The Upper Room Emmaus Ministries: Each program begins with several days spent in the company of the risen Christ, followed by a lifetime of Christian discipleship.

Speakers connect scripture stories with life experience.

As the two disciples walk to Emmaus, Jesus joins them as a stranger and explains to them the meaning of stories from his life. Likewise, stories from scripture and the experience of speakers are shared through presentations and discussions that address significant facets of God's grace and Christian discipleship.

Everyone experiences an atmosphere of grace.

Upon arrival in the village of Emmaus, the disciples recognize Jesus in the breaking of the bread; they remember how their hearts had burned within them as they walked with him on the road. Likewise, during an Emmaus Ministries event, grace is experienced through rich worship services, Holy Communion, the support of a caring Christian community, and other expressions of God's love.

Christian community is realized.

The disciples return immediately to the gathered community in Jerusalem to share their story and to hear their friends' stories of having seen the risen Christ. Likewise, during an Emmaus Ministries event, people live in Christian community and have opportunities to share their lives in fun-filled moments as well as serious moments, small-group discussions, singing, worship, and participation in the sacrament of Holy Communion.

THE EMMAUS MINISTRIES FAMILY AND THE UPPER ROOM

Emmaus Ministries includes programs for those seeking spiritual formation in several different life stages:

- **Chrysalis** serves secondary (high school) young persons fifteen to eighteen years old;
- **Journey to the Table** serves young adults eighteen to thirty-five years old;
- **Walk to Emmaus** serves adults eighteen years and older;
- **Face to Face** serves adults sixty years and older.

Origins of the Ministries

Traditionally, in Christianity, a "three-day movement" was a movement that conducted spiritual renewal events and was led by persons who had attended such an event. All such organizations were often collectively referred to as "three-day movements."

Most, but not all, of the events held by these organizations covered three days, and so the *Fourth Day* has become a term used by three-day movements to describe the life of the participant after the event.

The original three-day movement, Cursillo (cur-SEE-yoh), began in the Roman Catholic Church in Majorca, Spain, in 1944. Over time, Cursillo inspired the development of the Emmaus Ministries family of three-day movement programs.

Several resources provide information about the history of the Emmaus three-day movement and its relationship to Cursillo: *Day Four: The Pilgrim's Continued Journey*, *What Is Emmaus?*, and *The Early History of the Walk to Emmaus*.

In 1976, Danny Morris, Director of Developing Ministries for The Upper Room, participated in a Lutheran Cursillo in Florida and recognized the need for an ecumenical offering of Cursillo. On the same weekend, Maxie Dunnam, then World Editor of The Upper Room, participated in a prayer retreat at First United Methodist Church in Peoria, Illinois, where Cursillo participants contributed as table servants at the retreat. Their spiritual presence around the tables profoundly affected him.

Together, Danny and Maxie began to take steps toward including Cursillo as an Upper Room program. Under the leadership of Reverend Robert Wood, The Upper Room's first two model Cursillo weekends were held in Peoria, Illinois, in 1977. In 1978, Rev. Wood joined the staff of The Upper Room to launch the new Upper Room Cursillo movement.

In 1981, by mutual agreement with the National Secretariat of the Roman Catholic Cursillo, holder of the copyright to the Cursillo program, The Upper Room Cursillo became The Upper Room Walk to Emmaus. This change came about due to The Upper Room's call to be an ecumenical movement. The Upper Room reached an agreement with the National Cursillo Secretariat to develop a new program based on Cursillo but with distinctive leadership resources. Further, The Upper Room agreed not to use the traditional Cursillo language derived from its Spanish origin. The Upper Room developed The Walk to Emmaus design, talk outlines, and leadership manuals for use by an ecumenical audience.

Chrysalis began in 1984 in response to numerous requests from Emmaus Ministries Communities for a version of the Walk to Emmaus specifically for high school students. The Walk to Emmaus and Teens Encounter Christ (TEC)—the youth expression of the Roman Catholic Cursillo)—influenced the early development of Chrysalis. A group of Nashville high school youth attended TEC and acted as advisers to The Upper Room staff in creating a unique model and name for the program. And then, in 1989, The Upper Room and the Alabama/West Florida Emmaus Community sponsored the first Chrysalis event for college-age young people.

Face to Face, an adaptation of The Walk to Emmaus, was developed to meet the needs and life stages of older adults and those for whom an overnight experience presented a challenge. Development of the Face to Face program began in 2008, with the first Encounter being held in 2011 in a Nashville area church. In 2014, the first Encounter using the officially developed materials took place, and in 2015, Emmaus Ministries Communities outside the Nashville area began to hold Encounters.

Journey to the Table had its beginning in March of 2014, when The Upper Room established a new staff position for "Young Adult Spiritual Development." In September of 2014, the first five steering team leaders came to Nashville for three days of prayerful discussion and planning. After that meeting, an additional fourteen people joined working groups to write the first draft of the program. This group included young adults, campus ministers, and Emmaus and Chrysalis leaders. That draft of the new Journey to the Table program was completed in March of 2015, and five locations held test events in 2015 and 2016. The official launch of the program was held at The Upper Room in Nashville, Tennessee, in July 2016.

The Upper Room

The Upper Room, a division of Discipleship Ministries, an agency of The United Methodist Church, holds the copyright for all Emmaus Ministries programs. Therefore, it is important for Emmaus Ministries Communities to understand the nature of Upper Room Ministries and its role.

Upper Room Ministries

The Upper Room is a global ministry dedicated to supporting the spiritual formation of Christians seeking to know and experience God more fully. Upper Room Ministries is an interdenominational and international publisher and distributor of print and audiovisual resources and programs. The publishing and program ministries exist to encourage and guide people in a vital, intimate, and transforming relationship with God and to help them connect to the larger Christian community of faith.

Upper Room Ministries and The United Methodist Church

Upper Room Ministries is a division of the Discipleship Ministries agency of The United Methodist Church with responsibility for resourcing prayer and devotional life. Financially, Upper Room Ministries is unique in the Discipleship Ministries agency because of its self-supporting nature. While other divisions of the Discipleship Ministries agency and all other boards and agencies of the denomination depend upon World Service offerings, Upper Room Ministries depends on the sales revenues of Upper Room devotional literature.

Upper Room Publications, Print, and Electronic Resources

The Upper Room is best known for *The Upper Room* devotional magazine, which is the centerpiece of The Upper Room's ministry. This daily devotional guide is published in more than thirty languages and distributed in over one hundred countries with an estimated readership in the millions from many denominations and faith communities. Since its inception, the guide has aimed to enable and encourage Christian worship and devotion in the home. The Upper Room also publishes *Pockets*, a devotional magazine for children; *devozine*, a devotional magazine written for and by teens; *The Upper Room Disciplines*, an annual devotional book with meditations on scripture for every day of the year; and ten to fifteen new books each year on spiritual formation topics.

Upper Room Ministries also provides leadership and oversight in a variety of ongoing spiritual formation areas. In addition to the Emmaus Ministries programs, these include the following:

- *Academy for Spiritual Formation*® that shares commitment to an authentic spirituality that promotes balance, inner peace and outer peace, holy living and justice living, God's shalom.

- *Living Prayer Center,* a 7-days-a-week intercessory prayer ministry staffed by Christian volunteers.

- *eLearning* opportunities that seek to bring small groups together from around the world to read, reflect, and pray together.

- *Discovery Weekend* a spiritual formation weekend where younger youth experience God's love, the joy and forgiveness of Christ, and the gifts of the Holy Spirit.

Upper Room Ministries staff also work directly with churches or churches' governing bodies to help develop spiritual formation emphases according to the specific needs.

Upper Room Ministries' Role in Emmaus Ministries

Upper Room Ministries initiated The Upper Room Cursillo and later developed The Upper Room Walk to Emmaus and the other Emmaus Ministries programs. These copyrighted programs may be used only by permission of Upper Room Ministries. **Emmaus Ministries Communities enter into an annual written agreement to follow the Upper Room Ministries' guidelines and to maintain the programs according to these guidelines.**

Since the beginning of The Walk to Emmaus, Upper Room Ministries has underwritten the cost of its staffing and development and continues to assist in supporting its staff and operating budgets. Through the directors of the Emmaus Ministries Office, The Upper Room

- provides oversight of the Emmaus Ministries' expansion and development.

- upholds the quality standards by which Emmaus Ministries events and Emmaus Ministries Communities operate.

- interprets Emmaus Ministries to church leaders or church governing bodies in order to gain their support and involvement in Emmaus Ministries.

- serves as a center of information for those making inquiries about Emmaus Ministries and for persons involved in Emmaus Ministries who inquire about other Communities or events.

- sets policy for the Emmaus Ministries and Emmaus Ministries events.

- develops and publishes printed manuals and leadership resources for team formation and Emmaus Ministries events.

- resources and trains individuals from local Communities to facilitate training in every phase of Emmaus Ministries within the local Community.

- directs new groups and Steering Committees in the process of getting Emmaus Ministries started in new areas by meeting with Steering Committees, helping set up initial teams, and providing key leadership for the first events as needed.

- distributes an Emmaus Ministries e-newsletter to provide news about the expanding Emmaus Ministries and offers guidance and education through best practices about aspects of Emmaus Ministries.

- maintains a website at www.upperroom.org that provides current information about Emmaus Ministries activities and Communities.

- sponsors celebrations around the United States that offer education on various topics of Emmaus Ministries leadership, fellowship, meetings with Community members around the region, opportunities to receive current information about the status of Emmaus Ministries around the world, and learning sessions on other means of spiritual growth.

- trains persons in the Emmaus Ministries to provide leadership and training for other Emmaus Ministries Communities.

- sends representatives on behalf of Upper Room Ministries *when necessary* to provide Emmaus Ministries event leadership or training.

- responds to international inquiries for Emmaus Ministries and coordinates efforts to share Emmaus Ministries with the church beyond the United States.

- relates to other Fourth-Day organizations, such as Cursillo, including the Kairos Prison Ministry.

Funding for Emmaus Ministries

Each Community commits to share with Upper Room Ministries the financial burden of overseeing and resourcing the ministry:

- Local Communities commit to support the work of the Emmaus Ministries Office with payment as part of the annual Covenant Agreement. The Communities send a monetary offering to the Emmaus Ministries office after each event, set of events, or at the end of the year.

- Community leaders encourage donations to The Gift, a fund-raising initiative led by the Emmaus Ministries Office. It supports the work of emerging Communities around the world. People may also donate to the operating budget of Emmaus Ministries. These requests may come one or more times per year at Community Gatherings, by direct appeal to Community members, and/or by including donation information in Emmaus Ministries event participants' packets. Individuals can make a one-time donation, a monthly gift, or take part in a legacy giving plan.

INTRODUCTION TO EMMAUS MINISTRIES

Each of the Emmaus Ministries programs is designed to be an extraordinary act of love. In addition, the ministries share these elements:

- teaching of God's grace,
- partnership between lay and clergy leaders,
- celebration of Holy Communion,
- an experience of support from the community of believers,
- a sending forth with the understanding that Christ is counting on each of us,
- and a structure for progressive servanthood.

Most importantly, these ministries share an experience of people loving others into a deeper realization of God's love, supporting one another's decision to walk in the grace of Jesus Christ, and sacrificing to make this opportunity possible for others.

Purpose

Emmaus Ministries exists to inspire, challenge, and equip local faith communities for Christian action in their homes, churches, communities, and places of work. This purpose does not come to full realization for its participants during the Emmaus Ministries event itself but in the many days that follow.

Emmaus Ministries expands participants' spiritual lives, deepens their faith and discipleship, and rekindles—or perhaps ignites for the first time—their gifts as Christian leaders for their churches and communities. These aims are accomplished not only during the Emmaus Ministries event itself but also through participation in follow-up spiritual support groups and Community fellowship opportunities, sponsorship, prayer, support of other Emmaus Ministries events, and service on support committees and teams.

Persons whose spiritual lives are renewed and strengthened through Emmaus Ministries are called and empowered to be the hands and feet of Christ: to share within their communities the grace they received. They become energetic and renewing catalysts in their homes, places of work or education, and local communities of faith. While walking together with other Christians, they actively participate in God's mission to the world.

IMPORTANT FEATURES OF EMMAUS MINISTRIES PROGRAMS

All Emmaus programs share particular aspects, both theologically and systematically. These aspects provide a balanced and effective approach to spiritual growth.

Grounded in the Theology of Grace

The teachings and theology of John Wesley serve to ground all Emmaus Ministries. In Wesley's sermon *Free Grace,* preached in Bristol in 1740, he said that grace "does not in any wise depend either on the good works or righteousness of the receiver." In Wesley's understanding, believers who repent and accept Christ are not making themselves righteous by an act of will. This would alter the dependency of believers on the grace of God for salvation. Rather, through faith and repentance, believers trust that God will make them righteous—a gift freely bestowed by a loving God.

Ecumenical

Emmaus Ministries invites and involves the participation of Christians from many denominations and traditions. It is ecumenical, however, not only because of broad participation but also because Emmaus Ministries seeks to foster Christian unity and to reinforce the whole Christian community. Ecumenicity is one of the great strengths and joys of Emmaus Ministries.

A goal for each Emmaus Ministries event and for an Emmaus Ministries Community itself is for all involved to exhibit a spirit of openness and appreciation for the gifts of different Christian traditions and perspectives to gain strength from the ecumenism. This broadmindedness does not signal a theologically indifferent ministry. On the contrary, the very design of

Emmaus Ministries communicates with confidence and depth the essentials of Christian life, while accentuating the features Christians have traditionally held in common.

Quality Assurance

Each of The Upper Room's Emmaus Ministries programs is a carefully designed set of experiences conducted with discipline according to a universally standard handbook. Communities may offer Emmaus Ministries programs only with the permission and under the guidelines of The Upper Room. This covenant ensures a proven format and a common experience that will be trustworthy from event to event wherever a Community offers an Emmaus Ministries program.

The nature of Emmaus Ministries minimizes the dangers of building experiences around charismatic personalities or redesign according to the inclinations of individual leaders. Emmaus Ministries does not depend upon the exceptional gifts of any particular person and carefully avoids being leader-centered. A well-prepared team of people who work together in a spirit of love and servanthood conducts the Emmaus Ministries events and leads the Communities.

The Upper Room monitors and supports the quality of the movement and experiences offered by Emmaus Ministries Communities. The Upper Room's Emmaus Ministries Office provides guidance, training, and support for Emmaus Ministries Communities as needed. To ensure continued quality, the Emmaus Ministries Office expects a board and Community training event to be held every year within each local Community, led by persons trained and resourced by the Emmaus Ministries Office.

Scripturally Balanced

The Emmaus Ministries model unites knowledge and piety—the head and the heart—holding together the inward journey of personal piety and the outward journey of Christian action in the world. Emmaus Ministries also makes it clear, through both an event's talks and its communal experience, that personal Christian growth is not a solitary affair: Spiritual growth involves the support of other Christians and attention to relationships in the congregation and community. Finally, Emmaus Ministries stresses the importance of participation in Christian community, while also seeking to renew the body of Christ through a recovery of its spiritual tradition and openness to God's Spirit.

Laity and Clergy Involvement in Partnership

Emmaus Ministries makes laity and clergy partners in ministry. The intent is balance rather than dominance by either laity or clergy. The design fosters and models a partnership between clergy and laity in the work of the church, and both groups benefit from participation in this experience. Leadership roles on events and in the Community require both laity and clergy.

Commitment to Follow-up

From the outset, Emmaus Ministries designed its programs to be more than the event itself. It includes follow-up opportunities aimed at strengthening Christians' relationships with one another, supporting their growth as disciples, and encouraging their discipleship in the world through their Christian community. Emmaus Ministries continues to encourage persons to live as disciples through spiritual small groups (called group reunions or Next Steps groups) for mutual encouragement, continued spiritual growth, and accountability. The local Emmaus Ministries Community (and guests) come together regularly to fellowship and celebrate God's grace. These opportunities to share together in worship, prayer, and fellowship at the Emmaus Community level are called Gatherings.

The goal of Emmaus Ministries is to give persons the means to persevere in grace for the rest of their lives.

Effective

Often, participants exhibit a marked spiritual growth, and their behaviors and attitudes change as a result of their Emmaus Ministries experience—especially when they follow up their event with involvement in the regular meeting of a spiritual support group (called a group reunion or Next Steps group). People see the effects of Emmaus Ministries in the following areas:

- a greater awareness of the reality of God's love and a fresh commitment to Christ,
- emotional and relational healing,
- realization of persons' individual gifts in an atmosphere of Christian community,
- greater understanding of the Christian faith,
- desire to grow spiritually and make prayer and study part of their daily lives,
- a new sense of divine purpose and direction,
- readiness to share Christ's love in daily settings and in the greater community,
- awareness of the contradictions between the way life is and the world God intends,
- appreciation for the value of a faith community and the relevance of faith,
- new friendships with peers, younger or older persons, and clergy,
- greater dedication to Christian community,
- more eagerness to join study groups and service groups,
- more willingness to assume responsibilities,
- more appreciation for Christians who hold different perspectives,
- more meaningful involvement in worship and Holy Communion.

Time Apart from the World

All Emmaus Ministries programs ask participants to break from their usual routine in order to experience being in a Christian community of grace.

The Walk to Emmaus and Chrysalis events are cloistered. Participants stay on-site for the entire event under the spiritual direction of the Conference Room Team without the distractions of the outside world. Communities usually hold Walk to Emmaus and Chrysalis events in retreat centers or church facilities large enough to have kitchen and sleeping accommodations for about sixty people.

Face to Face lends itself to a less cloistered environment since participants do not stay overnight and can be hosted in 4-day or 8-day modules. Communities may offer Journey to the Table either in a cloistered residential setting or break the program into blocks in a less cloistered environment.

Relational

Emmaus Ministries values relationships. An Emmaus Ministries event provides a setting that encourages the formation of spiritual friendships that are often life-transforming and long-lasting. These relationships build on a shared experience of Christian love, faith, and spiritual growth.

All Emmaus Ministries foster positive intergenerational relationships. These relationships can begin intentionally in three ways: with team members of different generations during the event, in the community with people of different generations and programs, and in spiritual support groups and faith communities.

Personal Relationships

Emmaus Ministries does not exist for relationship enrichment or to facilitate communication between partners. However, even though they may attend events at different times or attend the same event but sit at different tables, married persons often find that these programs indirectly deepen their bond as partners in Christian relationship. While the Emmaus Ministries event is personal and unique for each of them, many couples embrace it as a shared spiritual touchstone through which they can respond and grow together.

Development of Leadership Skills

During the Emmaus Ministries event, participants may become aware of gifts and callings that can enrich their local faith community and their Emmaus Ministries Community. They can exercise their gifts through ongoing engagement in the Emmaus Ministries Community. They can strengthen public speaking and faith-sharing skills through involvement in spiritual support groups, Community Gatherings, and service on Emmaus Ministries event teams. They can explore various gifts of self-expression, organization, and management through work on the many volunteer committees that work together for the smooth operation of Emmaus Ministries Communities. As these skills develop over time, the servanthood model of Emmaus Ministries allows for progression into roles with increasing levels of leadership responsibilities. As these leadership skills develop, participants benefit the local faith community and other ministry organizations.

Spiritual Formation for Multiple Life Stages

The Upper Room offers multiple programs through the Emmaus Ministries to be in ministry with people in particular ways through a variety of life stages.

Chrysalis

Chrysalis is for secondary (high school) young persons, fifteen to eighteen years old. These years are a critical time in a person's spiritual formation. During this time, young people make major decisions about religion, lifestyle, vocation, and lifelong relationships. Chrysalis challenges them to grow not only in mind and body but also in spirit and faith.

The Chrysalis weekend events, which are referred to as Flights, are offered separately for girls and boys to allow youth freedom to explore their relationship with God without worrying about how they may appear to the other gender. It provides an opportunity outside their local congregations or youth groups to grow in their faith alongside their peers.

The butterfly provides the central image and metaphor of the Chrysalis experience. An ancient Christian symbol of Christ's death and resurrection, the butterfly illustrates one model of spiritual journey: caterpillar, cocoon (chrysalis), and butterfly. Dying to what it was, the caterpillar becomes what it is meant to be. Similarly, our Christian transformation involves dying with Christ to our old self through faith in God's accepting love; rising with Christ to a new life motivated by hope in God's promises; and going forth with Christ in love to joyfully share Christ's ministry of reconciliation and love with an alienated world.

Journey to the Table

Journey to the Table (JTT) is designed for young adults, eighteen to thirty-five years old—a time of life when young adults may find themselves moving to new community groups for school or work, navigating changing relationships, and taking on new responsibilities. Young adults are also developing a spiritual identity that is independent from the faith systems in which they may have grown up. The program offers a place to ask questions and encourages peers to share their experience and learning. It fosters an openness to how God and others may be working in their journey of faith. Journey to the Table provides an opportunity for young adults to explore their faith, build relationships, and create spaces of Christian action in a transitory time of life. Communities may host JTT as separate events by gender or with young adults all together. It consists of seven schedule blocks that include twenty-four hours of instructional time. Each location can choose to offer events either as an overnight, a continuous experience, or in any schedule using the seven schedule blocks. While Journey to the Table is a copyrighted program of The Upper Room, organizations other than an Emmaus Ministries Community may offer it (for example, in connection with a campus ministry).

The Walk to Emmaus

Walk to Emmaus is for adults eighteen years and older who are more established in a local church. Walk to Emmaus seeks to inspire, challenge, and equip adult leaders for Christian action in their homes, places of work, and communities.

In The Walk to Emmaus, an interdenominational group of forty to fifty people enters a unique communal experience. From Thursday evening until Sunday evening, the participants, or pilgrims, listen to fifteen talks that give a "short course" in Christian spirituality. They laugh and listen, worship and wonder, share and discuss. Many have testified to the life-giving experience of these three days.

The Walk to Emmaus follows the model of Cursillo in offering separate yet identical three-day experiences for males and females. Teams are selected according to the same model—male teams lead the events for males, and female teams lead the events for females. Clergy serving on these events will be a mix of both male and female.

The Walk supports this model for several reasons:

- It grants married persons time apart to explore their relationships with God without concern for their spouse's experience.

- It frees some spouses from patterns of behavior in their marriages that would prevent them from speaking openly about spiritual matters if they were together.

- It offers freedom for expression and sharing that some people do not feel in the presence of the opposite gender, whether participants are married or single.

Face to Face

Face to Face is an experience in the tradition of The Walk to Emmaus designed specifically for seniors, sixty years and older. The overarching theme is "Living in Grace."

The ages and physical circumstances of the Face to Face audience require several adjustments to The Walk to Emmaus model. The stamina of senior constituents and the scarcity of space in senior living communities dictate these adjustments. The adapted model presents the basic theological and biblical content of The Walk to Emmaus without the typical Walk format.

Face to Face consists of eight half-day sessions or four full-day sessions (scheduled over a period of two or more weeks). While most Walk to Emmaus talks are part of Face to Face, the program has added meaningful content for seniors. This content includes a talk given by a hospice representative or person who has lost a life partner and the video presentation of four meditations by United Methodist Bishop Rueben Job from his book and video series *Living Fully, Dying Well*.

Both men and women serve on the Face to Face team, and the event is open to both genders; however, table discussion groups are single gender.

In conclusion

Emmaus Ministries provides a safe place for participants to ask questions and explore beliefs or ideas. The programs invite participants to engage fully in their experience—listening and learning, participating in discussions and activities, and being open to how God and others may be working through the experience to travel with them on their journey of spiritual formation. In so doing, the participants become part of a larger community of faith, journeying together through the questions, blessings, and faith that each of us has in our lives.

SECTION 2— THE EMMAUS MINISTRIES COMMUNITY

An Emmaus Community is a recognized local group of Emmaus Ministries program participants (and possibly other "three-day movement" participants) in a geographic location. Each established Emmaus Community has signed a Covenant Letter with The Upper Room to present the Emmaus movement in its respective area and has accepted responsibility for doing so according to the terms of the agreement.

A group may start a new Emmaus Community by expressing a desire and obtaining adequate support within a location that is distant from other established Communities. While neighboring Emmaus Communities provide support in the process, new Emmaus Communities can be established only by The Upper Room Emmaus Ministries Office and according to Upper Room Emmaus Ministries conditions.

Once a new Community has met The Upper Room's requirements and is deemed ready to present an Emmaus Ministry event, a number of steps remain to plan, prepare for, and successfully conduct the Community's first Emmaus Ministry events. After hosting a sufficient number of Emmaus events, the Community will, with the assistance of The Upper Room Emmaus Ministries Office, transition its initial leadership to an elected governing body—a Board of Directors.

Under the guidance of its board, the Community continues to work with The Upper Room Emmaus Ministries staff in developing all aspects of Emmaus, including the addition of new Emmaus Ministry programs. This section provides information on the processes to follow to start

- a new Emmaus Community,
- an Emmaus Ministry program in a new or an established Community,
- an international Emmaus Community.

BEGINNING AN EMMAUS COMMUNITY

The process to begin a new Community involves the following:

- establishing a relationship with The Upper Room Emmaus Ministries Office;

- sponsoring sufficient numbers of persons to Emmaus events in established Communities to form a support Community;

- developing intentional Fourth Day (post-event) efforts with weekly group reunions, monthly Gatherings, and local church participation; and

- understanding that the Emmaus Ministries movement is much more than the events it conducts.

Before proceeding further, persons interested in starting the Emmaus movement in a new local area first contacts The Upper Room Emmaus Ministries Office. The proposed group will consider the following questions; the group's responses will allow The Upper Room to ascertain the propriety of establishing a new Community:

- What established Community will be the source for the new group?

- How long does it take to drive to the Emmaus events in the established Community?

- Does the established Community have a waiting list to attend Emmaus events?

- How many Emmaus events does the established Community conduct each year?

- Has the established Community been notified of the new group's intent?

- Does the established Community support the new group's becoming an Emmaus Community?

In the spirit of cooperation, the established "source" Community must commit support and assistance to the new Community's development, which would include the following:

- reserving spaces on each event for participants from the geographic area of the new Community;

- being intentional in providing Conference Room Team experience for qualified members of the new Community;

- offering members of the new Community's Steering Committee opportunities to sit in on board meetings of the established Community to gain perspectives on the board experience; and

- providing team leadership and experienced team members for the first events held by the new Community.

Requirements for a New Emmaus Community

A new group must meet several requirements before The Upper Room will consider it an Emmaus Community:

- The group has seventy-five to one hundred committed people who have participated in an Emmaus event.

- The group members have established themselves as a Fourth Day Community.

- Clergy who have completed an Emmaus event commit to support the new group.

- Clergy who have Conference Room Team experience pledge their support.
- The clergy willingly commit the time and effort to help establish the new Community.
- The new group commits to executing The Upper Room models for the Emmaus Ministries programs without importing flavors or traditions.

BEGINNING AN EMMAUS MINISTRY PROGRAM

After satisfying the initial requirements for a new Community, a proposed new Community begins its work toward readiness to offer Emmaus Ministries events. Typically, a new Community will plan to offer Walk to Emmaus events first to help quickly build up the Community with adults who can support and further the cause of the Emmaus movement in the new geographic area. A new Community may feel led to host a different Emmaus Ministry (such as Chrysalis, Face to Face) first. The Community decides in consultation with The Upper Room Emmaus Ministries Office.

For an established Emmaus Community, the time may come when it feels called to offer a new Emmaus Ministries program in addition to what it already provides.

For a new Community *and* an established Community, the decision to start an Emmaus Ministry program involves consideration of several factors and includes consultation with The Upper Room Emmaus Ministries Office to ensure a strong start to the ministry.

Starting with Strength

"Other seed fell into good soil and brought forth grain, growing up and increasing and yielding thirty and sixty and a hundredfold" (Mark 4:8).

Enthusiasm for Emmaus often brings with it the temptation to start an Emmaus Ministries program before considering important factors. Patience is indeed a proven virtue in starting an Emmaus Ministry program. Here are prerequisites for a strong beginning:

- adequate strength in the Emmaus Community,
- sufficient training or experience for those who will organize and lead the first events, and
- enough enthusiastic persons (the same age range as the participants) willing to serve on teams and to recruit and sponsor others.

Adequate Emmaus Community strength

Emmaus Communities that have a high level of maturity, stability, and respect for the original intent of The Walk to Emmaus have the greatest possibility of success when starting Emmaus Ministries program. All Emmaus Ministries depend on the leadership experience and resources of Emmaus-knowledgeable laity and clergy. A premature start can overextend the resources, human and otherwise, of some Emmaus Communities. This can harm the Emmaus Community, the new ministry, and the future relationship between the two.

Sufficient Leadership Training and Experience

Only Community members who bring sufficient knowledge and leadership experience from the Walk to Emmaus can hope to launch an additional Emmaus Ministries program with a measure of success. However, impatience to begin often tempts groups to minimize this need or to overestimate their leadership abilities, particularly if they do not have the necessary training and experience. Leaders must educate themselves in the new ministry by *reading the manuals*, observing ministry events in established Communities, participating on teams, and attending ministry training events offered by The Upper Room Emmaus Ministries. Ministry leaders who have taken these steps will find themselves generally equipped to organize and direct the new ministry teams through their first events.

Knowledge and experience for starting a new Emmaus Ministries program can also come from outside the Community from individuals who are active in established ministries. Neighboring Communities are often willing to help. Some Communities may need team members who bring an element of experience to the new event team. Others may need an event team leader (or other key team roles) who can model an approach to team formation and event leadership. In still other cases, the need may be for background support. In any of these cases, assign local team members to shadow and learn from the visiting team. The Upper Room Emmaus Ministries Office can recommend model Communities.

While help from other Emmaus Communities is always beneficial, that help can create a dependence on outside teams. If a Community can only host a new ministry event by importing visiting teams, it signals the Community's lack of readiness to launch the new ministry. First events are occasions for hands-on training of local people for future leadership. Without that experience, the Community's new ministry will remain dependent on visiting leaders. Team preparation for and participation in the first new ministry events also provide a critical test of a Community's commitment to the new ministry and its willingness to accept responsibility for its continuation. Seemingly successful events that rely on visiting teams can fail to launch a local Community's new ministry.

Enough Enthusiastic Participants

For an Emmaus Ministries program to take hold, the Emmaus Community, its leaders, and participants must catch the vision and want to share the experience with their friends and others. For this reason, the Emmaus Community and its leadership (Community Board or Steering Committee) need to give priority to ministry promotion, recruiting, and sponsoring. Sometimes this involves considerable travel and expense. But, in the end, we see participants who

* exhibit a sense of personal ownership of the program,
* are ready and excited to be ministry team members,
* are prepared to enthusiastically sponsor others to locally offered events, and
* are being blessed and becoming blessings in their faith communities, families, and the world.

We will then hear God say those cherished words, "Well done, good and faithful servant!" (Matt. 25:23, NIV).

Preparing for First Emmaus Ministries Events

Because the steps are similar, the list below will describe (1) the steps to be taken by a proposed new Community in preparation for its first ministry events, as well as (2) the steps to be taken by an established Community when starting a new Emmaus Ministries program. This process begins at least eighteen months prior to holding the first ministry event.

STEP 1: Pray.

- Begin praying for the Emmaus Ministries program that God wants to establish in your area, whether it is to be among youth, young adults, adults, or seniors.
- Consider the costs in time and energy for individuals and families, as well as the Emmaus Community.
- Discern God's call and seek to do only God's will.

STEP 2: Seek the Community's support.

- Look for confirmation of God's call in the commitment to the ministry expressed by others in the Emmaus Community.
- Make sure the Emmaus Community is willing to lead the ministry according to the direction and guidelines of The Upper Room Emmaus Ministries Office.
- Obtain a formal vote of commitment from the Emmaus Community Board to support the new ministry and its events (for an established Community adding a new ministry).

STEP 3: Establish a Steering Committee.

- *For a proposed new Community:* The group will form a Steering Committee and select a chair. Members of the Steering Committee must have leadership experience and be persons whose spiritual integrity will provide the proper foundation. The Steering Committee members will sit in as observers at board meetings of the established Community.
- *For an established Community adding a new ministry:* The Emmaus Community Board selects leaders and members for the new ministry's Steering Committee. Members of the Steering Committee must have leadership experience and be persons whose spiritual integrity will provide the proper foundation

Pray about the selection of these leaders; they will set the tone for the relationship with the Emmaus Community and the degree of attention Emmaus members will give to developing the new ministry's program.

The Steering Committee will consist of at least two members of the board and several (no more than ten) members of the established Community; if possible, the Steering Committee will include persons who have attended the new ministry elsewhere (such as Chrysalis youth).

A layperson (who has served effectively as a Walk to Emmaus Assistant Lay Director) and a clergyperson will lead the Steering Committee. The Emmaus Board selects them, and they serve at the will of the board.

STEP 4: Contact The Upper Room Emmaus Ministries Office.

- *For a proposed new Community:* The Steering Committee chair contacts The Upper Room Emmaus Ministries Office to request a visit. A representative of the Emmaus Ministries Office will come to the proposed group to meet and discuss the various aspects of being an Emmaus Community, including the Covenant Letter.

- *For an established Community adding a new ministry:* The Steering Committee leaders ask the sponsoring Community to prepare a letter requesting permission to develop the new ministry. The leaders send the letter, signed by the Community Lay Director and Community Spiritual Director, to The Upper Room Emmaus Ministries Office, P.O. Box 340004, Nashville, TN 37203-0004, ATTN: [Ministry Name] Program Manager.

STEP 5: Arrange for start-up training.

- *For a proposed new Community:* Following the initial visit, an Emmaus Ministries Office representative will contact the proposed Community to confirm a date for Community start-up training. An Upper Room-certified Emmaus trainer will conduct a Community training session and a board training session.

- *For an established Community adding a new ministry:* The Steering Committee will contact The Upper Room Emmaus Ministries Office and arrange for start-up training. The start-up training is for everyone involved in setting up the new ministry, including any board members who wish to participate and those on the first-event team(s). *The Team Selection Chair and Registration Chair are encouraged to attend.* The training is also open to all Community members, area clergy, and interested church members. It offers an opportunity to lay a foundation for understanding the new ministry and what is required to get it started.

STEP 6: Make a covenant with The Upper Room Emmaus Ministries Office.

- Every new Steering Committee signs a Covenant Letter with The Upper Room Emmaus Ministries Office before the Community offers an Emmaus Ministries program. The Upper Room Emmaus Ministries Office grants permission to use a copyrighted Emmaus Ministries program when a group demonstrates its readiness to lead the program under the conditions stated in the Covenant Letter. The Upper Room Emmaus Ministries Office is always involved in the process of establishing a new Emmaus Community and/or ministry, and establishes the standards by which the ministry will be led.

- Through its covenant with The Upper Room, the local Steering Committee agrees to keep faith with The Upper Room Emmaus Ministries Office by conducting Emmaus events in accordance with the Emmaus Ministries program materials.

- Each local governing body reviews and renews its Emmaus Ministries Covenant Letter with Upper Room Emmaus Ministries Office.
- *For an established Community adding a new ministry:* The leaders of the Steering Committee and the board that sponsors the new ministry signs the Covenant Letter. Formal support of the Community Board is required.

STEP 7: Choose leaders for the first event(s).

- The first events' team leaders are those respected as able and mature Christians with enough Emmaus leadership experience to organize the ministry. The Face to Face ministry requires leaders in the same age group as the participants—but not to the point of being exclusive.
- *For a proposed new Community:* When The Upper Room Emmaus Ministries Office staff agrees that the new group is ready to present its first Emmaus event(s), they will participate with the new group's Steering Committee in selecting the team leaders for the event(s).
- *For an established Community adding a new ministry:* The Emmaus Board may (1) select the first event's team leaders, (2) have the Team Selection Committee select them, or (3) have the ministry Steering Committee select them. In all cases, the board has final approval of the selected leaders.

STEP 8: Lay groundwork with church leaders.

- Build understanding of and support for the ministry among area church leaders. Ensure that the ministry has the affirmation and confidence of area United Methodist leaders and churches, as well as the affirmation and support of leaders and churches from other participating denominations.
- Reach out to youth pastors and other organized youth ministry efforts for Chrysalis; for Journey to the Table, contact campus ministries in the area; for Face to Face, seek out leaders of established senior ministries.

STEP 9: Observe and participate in ministry events in other Communities.

- The Upper Room Emmaus Ministries Office will help connect the Steering Committee with established Communities that can serve as examples and guide the committee in accordance with the ministry's Emmaus program model.
- Send potential ministry leaders to observe ministry events in established Communities. This immerses leaders in the dynamics of the ministry; they meet experienced leaders who can advise them.
- Encourage potential ministry leaders to gain Conference Room Team experience by volunteering to serve in an established Community.

STEP 10: Sponsor persons to attend events in other Communities.

- Sponsor participants at ministry events held by an established Emmaus Community. Intentionally sponsoring participants to attend events in other Communities during the start-up phase is crucial. Sponsorship builds ownership and enthusiasm in the ministry, as well as a sense of Community involvement from the outset. (This is particularly important for the Chrysalis ministry: The sponsored young persons can become the first youth team members and sponsors of other youth).

STEP 11: Select the venue for the event(s).

- The choice of venue will depend on the space requirements for the event, the dates of venue availability, the location of the venue, and the cost.
- Basic space requirements include a conference room large enough to accommodate up to sixty people around tables and a chapel (or large room that can serve as a chapel). Depending on the type of event (for example, Walk to Emmaus or Chrysalis), the requirements may also include sleeping space for up to sixty people and kitchen and dining facilities.
- Emmaus events are typically held in retreat centers or large church facilities; Face to Face events may also be held in retirement center facilities. Any venue must be fully accessible to persons with disabilities.
- For Face to Face, Emmaus Communities are encouraged to move subsequent events to different host organizations within the boundaries of the community, reaching out to the prospective pilgrims in the area and in surrounding churches and retirement centers.

STEP 12: Select the dates for the event(s).

- Seek dates that do not compete with other significant life and church activities.
- Consider weekends that border holidays or in-service days for teachers for Chrysalis so youth do not miss a day of school to attend the Chrysalis event.
- Decide whether the events will be separate or simultaneous if the ministry is offered as "pairs" of events (for men and for women). For simultaneous events, the men's and women's events are held on the same dates but in separate facilities or separate conference rooms in the same facility.
- Decide whether the men's or women's event will be held first when choosing separate events. For Walk to Emmaus, the men's event is usually held first. For Chrysalis, the girls' event is often held first, followed by the boys'; this practice is based on the assumption that, following their event, girls more actively encourage the boys to participate. These decisions are up to the local Community.
- Journey to the Table and Face to Face events can include both men and women on the same event and therefore do not require pairs of events.

STEP 13: Develop a recruitment/sponsorship plan for the event(s).

- Design a recruitment or promotion plan for the area, taking into consideration its unique characteristics. Pray for guidance and grace in these efforts.

- Educate the Community in the purpose, practice, and responsibilities of recruitment and sponsorship. At Community meetings, give people time to make sponsorship plans, to share them with one another, and to pray over them.

- Use the promotional/recruitment model for the Face to Face ministry. Sponsorship is not required, but it is not discouraged. Educate the Community in the ministry's promotional efforts and encourage members' assistance. Order the ministry brochures, and use the online promotional materials and other resources provided by The Upper Room Emmaus Ministries available at (http://facetoface.upperroom.org/resources) to develop your plan.

- Seek to sponsor (in the first event) those whose participation will encourage others to attend: strong laypersons, respected clergy (both male and female), church leaders, persons from various ethnic groups, persons committed to the church, and persons who represent a healthy and balanced spirituality.

- Seek to sponsor for Chrysalis two or more friends from particular churches and schools so they can attend together and encourage others.

- Set aside funds for scholarships.

- Have a minimum of twenty confirmed registrations. If the Community has fewer than twenty confirmed registrations two weeks prior to the event, then postpone the event.

- *For a proposed new Community:* intentionally recruit and sponsor. Especially for these first events, faithfully recruit persons who are vital, strong members and leaders in their churches whose participation will strengthen the launching of the Emmaus movement in your area.

STEP 14: Seek Emmaus Community support throughout the process.

- Do everything possible to build understanding of the ministry within the entire Emmaus Community (newsletters, email campaigns).

- Involve the Emmaus Community in praying and providing for the ministry's events in tangible ways, especially in sponsorship and/or promotional activities. Your Community members can be your greatest resource in reaching others within the targeted geographic area. Avoid letting the new ministry become a fringe activity in the Emmaus Community.

- Release unrealistic expectations that *all* Emmaus Community members will actively involve themselves in the new ministry.

STEP 15: Select and prepare team members for the event(s).

- *For a proposed new Community:* The Steering Committee begins to form the first teams approximately five months before the events with the assistance of the staff of The Upper Room Emmaus Ministries Office.

- *For an established Community adding a new ministry:* Team selection follows the ongoing process guidelines detailed in the "Teams" section of this document. For the first ministry events, the Emmaus Board may choose to have team selection handled by the established Community Team Selection Committee; or they may choose to have the ministry Steering Committee act as the Team Selection Committee. In either case, the acting Team Selection Committee works with the event's team leaders to select the remainder of the team.

- Team leaders take responsibility for providing team members with the materials and guidance needed to perform their tasks. The Upper Room Emmaus Ministries Office provides materials to aid team leaders in the all-important task of building and preparing the team in the months leading up to the ministry event. Again, refer to the "Teams" section of this document for in-depth instructions.

- For the Face to Face ministry, the Steering Committee leaders (Steering Committee Laity Leader and Clergy Leader) serve as Lead Coach and Spiritual Director on the first few events.

STEP 16: Develop a follow-up plan.

- Have a follow-up plan in place to support the new ministry's participants after their events *before* the first ministry events occur.

- *For a proposed new Community:* Assign a Steering Committee member the responsibility for follow-up—assisting with the formation of group reunions and planning Gatherings. Do not wait for the first events to take place before encouraging group reunions and holding Gatherings among local Emmaus pilgrims.

STEP 17: Transition the Steering Committee to a Board.

- *For a proposed new Community:* After a sufficient number of ministry events have been successfully held, representatives of The Upper Room Emmaus Ministries Office will assist the Steering Committee in transitioning to an elected governing body: a Board of Directors (Working Board) of the local Emmaus Community. The Steering Committee serves as the Nominating Committee for the election of the first board. See "Making the Transition from a Steering Committee to a Board of Directors" in the "Community Board of Directors" section below.

  The new board continues to work with Upper Room Emmaus Ministries staff in developing all aspects of its Emmaus ministry, in supporting the Emmaus movement in other areas with agape, and in relating to the Emmaus Ministries' International Advisory Committee.

- *For an established Community adding a new ministry:* Over the first several ministry events, the ministry Steering Committee works with the Emmaus Board to establish the management of the new ministry within the existing board structure. During this time, the ministry Steering Committee remains an active committee of the existing Emmaus Board.

- Once the new ministry is well-established, the initial ministry Steering Committee transitions to a Ministry Area Board, and the existing Emmaus Board transitions to a Governing Board/Ministry Area Board Structure. See the "Community Board of Directors" section below for descriptions of these board options and structures.

KEEPING FAITH WITH THE EMMAUS PROGRAM MODELS

By participating in any of these ministries when offered, the Community shares in a common experience with participants and teams around the world. Communities that remain healthy and fruitful over time demonstrate a commitment to this shared experience. This commitment helps leaders focus on the basics of providing a spiritual formation experience, and helps connect everyone involved through their shared experience. Persons can sponsor family and friends in other states, even in other countries, with confidence that the quality of the event will be the same in each location.

The Upper Room Emmaus Ministries Office works with a Vision Team of experienced leaders in these ministries to review and revise the manuals. When Communities envision a new or revised element of one of these ministries, please consult with The Upper Room Emmaus Ministries Office.

Being faithful to The Upper Room Emmaus Ministries' program manuals is critical to the ongoing quality and effectiveness of Emmaus programs for the following reasons:

- It prevents redesign by each leader.

  Adherence to the manuals prevents individual leaders from redesigning Emmaus events according to their whims. Unlike many religious events, Emmaus is not leader-centered: Its effectiveness does not depend on particular charismatic personalities, gifted presenters, or experienced retreat masters. No one asks, when invited to attend an Emmaus event, who the leader and speakers will be. Rather, Emmaus depends on a team of committed Christians working together in the spirit of Christ according to directions in objective manuals based on a proven model. The event team leaders for each Emmaus event are accountable to the local Emmaus Board, and the local board covenants with Upper Room Emmaus Ministries to lead the events according to the manuals.

- It assures consistent quality and common experience.

  The manuals ensure that Emmaus, no matter where it is conducted, will be a common and trustworthy experience. Church leaders in one part of a country can recommend Emmaus events to church leaders in another part of the country, knowing that the design and standards are uniform everywhere. This uniformity strengthens the Emmaus movement and its value to the church.

- It honors the integrity of the sponsors.

  Persons come to an Emmaus event trusting others' recommendation that Emmaus will be worth their time and will be conducted according to a certain design. Therefore, Emmaus leaders honor sponsors' faith that the event team will offer the program's model in its integrity.

- It preserves an organic model.

The Emmaus manuals set forth program models in which all parts are theologically and dynamically congruent. All Emmaus events are tightly woven. The models have proven their value and effectiveness time and again as instruments of the Holy Spirit in the lives of the participants and the churches to which they belong. Every part of the models has its purpose in this regard. When leaders rearrange a program model, adding some parts and deleting others, they increasingly diminish the model's potential for working as a whole to communicate the Christian message on many levels.

- It serves as a shared and stabilizing discipline.

Commitment to the manuals is a shared discipline that serves as a check on the inclination of team members to innovate and tinker with the design. In truth, most additions and changes are made for the team, not the participants. Team leaders may be motivated by a desire to replicate a spontaneous happening from a previous event or to add an experience from a retreat they once attended. Or they may get bored with the same routine and desire to try out a few ideas of their own. Some leaders have a gift for designing learning experiences and retreats; they may feel confident that they can improve Emmaus Ministries programs, given an opportunity.

Emmaus Ministries programs, however, already include more content than any participant can absorb over the course of the event; they offer enough material to meditate on for several years. Emmaus Ministries programs do not need to include every meaningful experience, interesting retreat idea, or variation from other spiritual events. Nor can Emmaus Ministries expand to meet every need in a participant's life. The church and the Emmaus Fourth Day follow-up activities provide other opportunities for spiritual renewal that can creatively support and challenge a participant's faith. Not everything that is meaningful has to happen during the Emmaus Ministries event itself.

- It channels creativity appropriately.

The manuals encourage leaders to focus their creativity on the given tasks within the Emmaus Ministries models. The place for creativity is not in redesigning the models but in making the most of the given designs to prepare the way of the Lord for the participants. The structure of Emmaus Ministries does not crowd out the Holy Spirit. Rather, it creates trustworthy space for the Holy Spirit to work in the midst of participants by eliminating anxiety about the weekend design and relaxing the focus on leaders. Acceptance of the models and manuals frees the event teams to focus on the participants and to trust the Holy Spirit.

In addition, changes by independent-minded team members set a dangerous precedent. While their innovations may work, future teams will want to claim their right to be creative as well and to try out their own ideas. Even more serious, changes become traditions overnight because new Emmaus Community members believe their experience represents the true Emmaus model. The manuals are the plumb line that keeps each event centered on the prescribed program.

- It prevents conflict over the event design.

    The discipline of adhering to the manuals frees the Emmaus Board and teams to focus their energies in the proper direction—on preparing for Emmaus events and Fourth Day challenges. Well-designed and carefully tested programs with complete materials for leading them is a gift that frees Emmaus Communities to get on with the business at hand.

- It enables Emmaus Communities to participate more fully in the larger Emmaus movement.

    Emmaus Communities that are grounded in The Upper Room Emmaus Ministries models have the privilege and ability to be asked to work with The Upper Room Emmaus Ministries to help start new Emmaus groups and ministries. The Upper Room Emmaus Ministries Office seeks Emmaus leaders and Communities that know and practice the Emmaus Ministries models and want to help spread Emmaus in a trustworthy and dependable manner.

- It honors the covenant with The Upper Room Emmaus Ministries.

    The manuals warrant adherence because an Emmaus Community exists through a covenant with The Upper Room Emmaus Ministries Office. As a condition of that covenant, each Emmaus Community agrees to follow the manuals. No doubt, other practices, including other three-day movement experiences, are rich and meaningful. Affirming the Emmaus models does not negate the validity of other promising experiences. However, if a group has decided to be an Emmaus Community, then that decision dictates that the Community be true to its identity and present the distinctive Emmaus Ministries models. Emmaus Communities function under the banner of The Upper Room Emmaus Ministries and are responsible for doing so in a manner faithful to the conditions of that relationship.

- Change should be in the direction of moving closer to The Upper Room model.

    Each Emmaus Community has its own personality and style. The Upper Room Emmaus Ministries Office will work with international Communities based on their cultures to ensure that they adhere to the basic Emmaus model. Minor differences will exist among some Communities because of their regions and background in starting. This will always be the case and is more noticeable in some areas than in others. But the direction of change for an Emmaus Community's models should always be in the direction of the standard Upper Room Emmaus Ministries models, not away from them.

The appropriate way to channel concerns and suggestions for improving the basic Emmaus programs' models and manuals is through The Upper Room Emmaus Ministries Office and the Emmaus Ministries Vision Team. The Vision Team consists of experienced, grassroots Emmaus Ministries leaders from Communities across the Emmaus movement. Emmaus Communities work with The Upper Room Emmaus Ministries Office to make improvements based on adequate understanding of and experience with the basic Emmaus

Ministries models. Each Emmaus Community functions beyond its local group; each Community is part of a larger Emmaus Ministries movement.

BEGINNING AN INTERNATIONAL EMMAUS COMMUNITY

Starting an international Emmaus Community presents a new series of challenges and thus requires a different set of strategies. As a first step, the ecclesial authority of the proposed international Community would submit a letter of invitation to The Upper Room Emmaus Ministries Office. Exchange of information and possibly a visit with the ecclesial authority may follow. Once these two entities have established written agreement, the development process can begin.

Developing international Communities warrants special care. Language considerations and cultural considerations require careful exploration within the context of The Upper Room Emmaus Ministries models. Monetary considerations have to be evaluated. While one model may work in one setting, another setting may need a different model.

All international initiatives must be processed through The Upper Room Emmaus Ministries Office. Experience has demonstrated that one key element in the successful start-up and effective continuation of international Communities has been the relationship established between The Upper Room Emmaus Ministries Office and the appropriate ecclesial authority.

COMMUNITY BOARD OF DIRECTORS

The local Emmaus Board of Directors is the body that governs the local Emmaus movement and oversees the quality of the program. The Board of Directors links the local Emmaus Community with The Upper Room Emmaus Ministries and is responsible for fulfilling the covenant with Upper Room Emmaus Ministries Office as stated in the Covenant Letter. Detailed information about the Board of Directors, responsibilities of board members, and accountability functions of the board can be found in the book *The Board of Directors*.

Making the Transition from a Steering Committee to a Board of Directors

After a new Community's first few Emmaus Ministries events, its Steering Committee acts as a Nominating Committee to nominate persons to fill fifteen positions on the board. The newly elected board may consist of three classes with four laypersons and one clergyperson in each class. Characteristics of nominees include maturity and experience for guiding this new Community, as well as an ability to work with others in a cooperative manner. The new board will consist of sixteen (16) members, twelve lay and three clergy, plus a Clergy Leader of the Emmaus Community. The newly elected board then selects the Clergy Leader from among all clergy participants in an Emmaus event.

Those nominated for election to the board need to understand that the Emmaus Board is a working board. The only privilege of being on the board comes in serving to further the Emmaus movement and fulfill its objectives.

Everyone who has participated in an Emmaus event receives a ballot by whatever means will get the ballot into the most hands within the Community. Give respondents an ample amount of time to return their ballots. The Nominating Committee receives and counts the ballots.

The Steering Committee chair or another Steering Committee member who was not nominated to be on the new board convenes the newly elected board.

The new board's first order of business is to select from among themselves a Board Chair who becomes the Community Lay Director. The newly elected Board Chair then conducts the remainder of the organizational meeting.

The board's second order of business is to elect a Community Spiritual Director who will serve as the sixteenth member of the board. All clergy who have participated in an Emmaus event, including those already elected to the board, are eligible for selection. If a newly elected clergy member of the board is selected to serve as Community Spiritual Director, then another clergyperson who was a runner-up in the election can fill the vacated position. Communities avoid this problem in the future by the board's electing the Community Spiritual Director each year prior to the annual nominations process and board elections.

The board's third order of business is to form three classes. The chair conducts a drawing among the board members to determine who will be in each class. Those who draw a one-year term will be eligible for renomination and reelection for a new three-year term at the end of the first year.

The board's fourth order of business is to assign board members responsibilities for standing committee tasks. The chair, in conversation with the board members about board responsibilities, appoints each of the fifteen elected members as chair of one of the standing committees listed in Article VII of the bylaws.

A Working Board

In most cases, the Emmaus Ministries Office recommends that the local Board of Directors be set up in this way:

1. The Board of Directors consists of three classes of five persons, a new class being elected each year, and the oldest class rotating off. In addition, the Board of Directors annually selects the Community Spiritual Director, a voting member of the board. The number of positions on the board is based on the number of ongoing tasks that require leadership to enable the Emmaus Ministries events and to support the Community.

2. The Emmaus Community elects the board by voting each year on members of a new class from among nominees selected by a Nominating Committee and approved by the board. Voting ballots are mailed or distributed through an electronic means that will guarantee one person, one vote.

3. Each person on the board chairs one of the committees needed to support the ministry events and follow-up. These committees serve many functions, one of the most

fundamental being leadership development. Find helpful information about this function in the book *The Board of Directors*.

4. Board meetings are held once a month.

5. The immediate past Lay Director (chair) of the board serves on the board the next year in a consulting position without vote.

6. The board has a Team Selection Committee (or Team Selection Committee Chair) and a Nominating Committee.

7. Board members do not serve on Conference Room Teams during their terms on the Board of Directors. The exception is the Board Representative for each team.

8. The board annually elects officers consisting of Lay Director (chair of the board), Spiritual Director, Secretary, Treasurer, and other officers as needed from among its own members. In addition to these board officers, each of the board members has a specific assignment for supporting the ministry events and maintaining the health of the Emmaus Community. Each is called a committee chair and is empowered to organize a committee of non-board Community members as needed in order to accomplish the task. These standing committees for which each board member serves as chair include the following: Team Selection, Registration, Transportation, Facility and Set-up, Agape Acts, Kitchen, Literature, Music, Sponsors' Hour, Entertainment, Candlelight, Group Reunions, Gatherings, Newsletter, Outreach, and Other Ministries. The chair, in conversation with the board members about board responsibilities, appoints each of the fifteen elected members as chair of one of the standing committees.

9. The Community Spiritual Director is elected annually by consensus of members of the Emmaus Community Board. The election of the Community Spiritual Director precedes the regular board elections by the Community and coincides with the nominations process. In this way, the board will not need to fill a position on the board in case a clergyperson on the board is selected as its Community Spiritual Director. The Nominating Committee can take these factors into account when considering persons to fill vacancies. The Community Spiritual Director is elected annually. The board determines the number of years a clergyperson can serve in this position.

The list above is the design of a Working Board of twelve to fifteen persons. This board structure relieves the team leaders of concern for innumerable tasks in preparation for ministry events and frees them to focus on team formation and the event itself. Board members assume responsibility for enabling the predictable support functions for every event, such as kitchen help, table agape, facility set-up, entertainment, clergy leadership for Candlelight, as well as Community functions such as Gatherings and follow-up to encourage group reunions. A board member's responsibility may change each year or remain the same from one year to the next. When a board member's committee responsibility changes, the chair makes every effort to encourage the person relinquishing the responsibility to train the person assuming that responsibility. This training provides for smooth transitions from one committee leader to another.

Board Responsibilities

The board sets a regular meeting date, discusses the status of each board member's area of responsibility, and considers the need for a Community training day to help everyone grow in his or her understanding of Emmaus leadership.

Each Community conducts a board training session soon after the election of the board officers. This training will provide orientation for the board members and will assist each board member in the efficient handling of his or her responsibilities. This board training is held as an annual event following the assumption of duties by new board members. A helpful guide for this training is the book *The Board of Directors*.

Each board establishes the minimum number of confirmed registrations to allow an Emmaus event to go forward. The recommended minimum is twenty (20) confirmed registrations at least two weeks prior to the event dates.

Community Lay Director's Responsibilities

1. The Community Lay Director chairs the Board of Directors and is elected annually by the board from among returning board members to serve during the upcoming year.

2. The Community Lay Director, with the help and support of the Spiritual Director, oversees and orchestrates the activities of the Emmaus Community. The Community Lay Director plans and conducts board meetings and makes sure board members follow through on their assignments.

3. The Community Lay Director represents a mature understanding of the Emmaus movement, the Emmaus Ministries programs, and team formation in order to help the board make decisions that ensure that Emmaus is of high quality and a positive influence in the life of the Christian community.

4. When unusual problems arise in team formation or during Emmaus Ministries events that seriously threaten the possibility or integrity of the event according to the Community and Upper Room Emmaus Ministries standards, the board takes responsibility to make decisions about the situation. If that is not possible, the Community Lay Director can act with the Spiritual Director and the Board Representative on the team to consult with team leaders in Christian love and help them evaluate their leadership in relation to their commission from the board. In such unusual circumstances, the Community Lay and Spiritual Directors can make decisions as needed on behalf of the board. The Community Lay Director never unilaterally or arbitrarily interferes with the appointed leadership of an Emmaus Ministries event or with its efforts to carry out assigned responsibilities.

5. The Community Lay Director participates in Closings of Emmaus Ministries events, as indicated in the Closing agenda, by welcoming the event participants to the Emmaus Community, announcing upcoming Emmaus activities, and presenting the team leaders for the next event(s). If the Community Lay Director cannot be present, then he or she makes sure an appropriate lay leader on the Emmaus Board undertakes this.

6. The Community Lay Director represents the Emmaus Community to the broader Emmaus Ministries Community.

7. The Community Lay Director carries out his or her responsibilities in a spirit of teamwork with the Board of Directors.

Community Spiritual Director's Responsibilities

1. The Community Spiritual Director is elected annually by the board to be a member of the Board of Directors of the Emmaus Ministries Community. The board selects this person from among the clergy who have participated in the Emmaus movement in that Community.

2. The Community Spiritual Director acts as spiritual leader of the Emmaus Ministries Community and helps the board remain centered on Jesus Christ, focused on the purpose of the Emmaus movement, and aware of God's presence in the decision-making process. The Community Spiritual Director pays special attention to the spiritual atmosphere and health of the Emmaus Ministries Community; the theological soundness of the Emmaus events; and the quality of the fruit born of Emmaus in churches, homes, and community in light of the intended goals of Emmaus Ministries.

3. The Community Spiritual Director meets with every clergyperson who attends an Emmaus event to discussion the person's perspectives on Emmaus, background, interest in Emmaus, and how he or she might serve the Emmaus Ministries Community, including possible service as an assistant team leader and potentially a team leader.

4. The Community Spiritual Director recommends to the board qualified clergy who could serve well as team leaders, although the board is not limited to his or her recommendations. To serve the board effectively in this regard, the Community Spiritual Director keeps up with clergy participation in events and on teams and is prepared to help the Team Selection Committee select and cultivate clergy leadership.

5. The Community Spiritual Director participates in the Team Selection Committee process of selecting team members for upcoming events, especially for the purpose of helping select clergy for the teams. The Community Spiritual Director maintains a list of all qualified clergy within the Emmaus Ministries Community.

6. The Community Spiritual Director contacts the board's selection of clergy team leader for an upcoming team and secures his or her acceptance.

7. The Community Spiritual Director orients and prepares the upcoming clergy team leaders for their role in team formation and the Emmaus Ministries events as needed. Team responsibility may require the Community Spiritual Director to present an overview of the Emmaus event, the standards by which the team conducts the event, and the spirit of the team's participation during the first team meeting or team orientation meeting. The overview and standards establish continuity from one team to the next in their approach.

8. When unusual problems arise, either in team formation or during Emmaus Ministries events, that seriously threaten the possibility or integrity of the event according to the Community and Upper Room Emmaus Ministries standards, the board takes responsibility to make decisions about the situation. If that is not possible, the Community Spiritual Director can act with the Community Lay Director and the Board Representative on the team to consult with team leaders in Christian love and help them evaluate their leadership in relation to their commission from the board. In such unusual circumstances, the Community Spiritual and Lay Directors can make decisions as needed on behalf of the board. The Community Spiritual Director never unilaterally or arbitrarily interferes with the appointed leadership of an event or with its efforts to carry out assigned responsibilities.

9. The Community Spiritual Director presents the Emmaus cross to the event lay team leader at the Closing of each Emmaus event on behalf of the Community. The Community Spiritual Director also leads the Holy Communion service during the Closing of each event. When the Community Spiritual Director cannot fulfill these roles, he or she makes certain an appropriate clergyperson, such as the clergy event team leader, undertakes them.

10. The Community Spiritual Director represents and interprets the Emmaus movement at its best among clergy colleagues and church leaders and encourages their participation on events and teams and their leadership in the Emmaus Community. The Community Spiritual Director shares with clergy colleagues the Emmaus experience and the value of the Emmaus movement to the church. The Community Spiritual Director will offer to sponsor or will arrange for a sponsor for his or her colleagues.

11. The Community Spiritual Director carries out his or her responsibilities in a spirit of teamwork with the Board of Directors.

SAMPLE BYLAWS AND BOARD STRUCTURES

Each new Board of Directors will adopt bylaws that set forth the structure and rules of operation for the board. The following bylaws model those used by many Emmaus Communities. A new Community could adopt them as they are or adapt them as needed.

Each Community reviews the bylaws every five (5) years. This review assures that the Board of Directors functions in accordance with its own mandates and provides the board the opportunity to make necessary revisions in the bylaws to reflect current practice.

Explanatory information about the bylaws can be found in the section titled "Governing Documents" of the book *The Board of Directors*.

Typical Bylaws for an Emmaus Ministries Community

ARTICLE I. NAME

The name of this Community shall be The _____ Emmaus Community, hereinafter referred to as the Community.

ARTICLE II. PURPOSE

Section 1. The purpose of the Community shall be to inspire, challenge, and equip church members for Christian action in their homes, churches, places of work, and the world community through the Emmaus experience.

Section 2. The Community is affiliated with The Upper Room Emmaus Ministries Office, Nashville, Tennessee.

ARTICLE III. MEMBERSHIP

Section 1. All persons who have completed an Emmaus Ministry event sponsored by an Upper Room Emmaus Community shall be members of the Community.

Section 2. Persons who have completed a recognized three-day movement experience may become members by participating in the activities of the Community and asking the secretary or registrar of the Community to include their names on the mailing list.

ARTICLE IV. BOARD OF DIRECTORS

Section 1. Purpose

Direction of the Community shall be vested in a Board of Directors.

Section 2. Composition

The Board will consist of fifteen (15) elected lay members and the Community Spiritual Director.

Section 3. Terms of Office

  a) Laypersons on the board shall be elected by the Community members for three (3)-year terms in three (3) classes, each class having five (5) members.

  b) Board members cannot succeed themselves in consecutive terms, a term being three (3) years.

  c) Terms of office shall begin January 1 and shall terminate December 31, except for officers who shall serve until election of new officers in January as provided in Article V.

Section 4. Election of Board Members

  a) Board members are elected by the Community.

  b) The Nominating Committee shall submit to the board a slate of seven (7) nominees from which to elect five (5) board members.

  c) The ballot shall be provided to the Community members in the most effective way possible and shall be available no later than October 15 of each year.

  d) Ballots are to be received by the board no later than November 15 of each year.

  e) Election is by majority vote of the ballots cast.

f) The immediate past chair of the board shall serve on the board one (1) additional year or the normal period of the term, whichever is longer.

g) The board may elect persons, upon nomination by the chair, to fill a vacant term until the next regular election for that term. Such persons are eligible for election to a full term by the Community at such regular election.

ARTICLE V. OFFICERS OF THE BOARD

Section 1. Officers

Officers shall be the Chair, Vice-Chair, Secretary, and Treasurer; and in case of absences will chair meetings in this order. The vice-chair must be eligible to serve an additional year on the board and serve as the chair if elected to that post. Officers may accept responsibility for a work area in addition to an elected position on the board.

Section 2. Election of Officers

Officers shall be elected annually by the Board of Directors at the January meeting for a one (1)-year term of office effective with the close of the January meeting.

Section 3. Spiritual Director

The Spiritual Director of the Community shall be selected annually by the Board of Directors. Term of office shall begin January 1. The Spiritual Director may be replaced during the term by ten (10) affirmative votes.

ARTICLE VI. MEETINGS

Section 1. The board shall meet monthly in regular meetings unless otherwise ordered by a two-thirds (2/3) vote of the board in a regular meeting.

Section 2. Quorum

Ten (10) members of the Board of Directors present at a duly called meeting shall constitute a quorum.

Section 3. Special Meetings

Special board meetings may be called by the chair or when requested in writing by ten (10) members of the board.

ARTICLE VII. COMMITTEES

Section 1. The Board of Directors shall name board members to chair the following committees: Gatherings, Registration, Transportation, Facility Set-Up/Breakdown, Agape Acts, Group Reunions/Follow-Up, Kitchen, Literature/Clothing, Team Selection, Newsletter, Other Ministries, Music/Entertainment, Candlelight/Sponsors' Hour, and Community Training.

Section 2. The chair of the board will be an ex-officio member of all standing committees.

ARTICLE VIII. WALK TO EMMAUS

Section 1. The Community shall follow the guidelines of The Upper Room Emmaus Ministries programs in the presentation of any Emmaus Ministries event. The guidelines are attached hereto.

Section 2. The Board of Directors shall have general oversight in all matters relating to the local Emmaus Ministries Community.

Section 3. The Board of Directors shall choose an event lay team leader for each Community Emmaus Ministries event.

Section 4. The Board of Directors shall choose an event clergy team leader for each Community Emmaus Ministries event.

Section 5. The board shall establish a Team Selection Committee. The Team Selection Committee shall consist of a board member who serves as chair, the Community Spiritual Director, and three (3) [or four (4)] members of the Emmaus Community who have broad awareness of the Community membership and a solid understanding of team needs. Community members are appointed by the board chair.

ARTICLE IX. AMENDMENTS

Section 1. Proposed amendments may be presented to the board by any member of the Community one (1) month in advance for consideration by the board.

Section 2. If the amendments are voted in the affirmative by a three-fourths (3/4) vote of the board, they will be circulated to the membership through the Community newsletter and if no petitions signed by at least twenty-five (25) Community members objecting to the new amendments are received, the amendments will be considered adopted. Any objections must be received within sixty (60) days of the mailing of the notification. If an objection petition is received, the amendment will be considered void.

Section 3. If the board then wishes to submit the amendment to the entire Community for a vote, it may do so. A majority or plurality of votes cast by the membership will decide the matter.

ARTICLE X. RATIFICATION

The bylaws take effect immediately upon certification of the board that a majority of the mail ballot of the Community approves them.

Types of Boards

Depending on how many events/ministries an individual Community is hosting, the type of board needed may change. As the Community starts new programs or recognizes the need to change the way the Community is managed, the board investigates and makes recommendations on what type of board is needed. With the exception of the Community/Ministry Area Lay Director and the Community/Ministry Area Spiritual Director, the exact job descriptions for these positions are a task for the local Community (for an understanding of the Ministry Area designation, see the Governing Board description).

The board choices are these:

Working Board (previously discussed in this section)—for Communities hosting one to two sets of events annually,

Coordinating Board—for Communities hosting 3 or more sets of events annually,

Governing Board—for Communities running 2 or more Ministry Areas (Chrysalis, Face to Face, etc.).

Coordinating Board

When an Emmaus Board of Directors oversees more than three sets of Emmaus Ministries events per year held in several sites covering a large geographic area, the may choose to have a Coordinating Board. The events may be too many or too far removed for the board members to resource effectively each event or each constituent area's Fourth Day. The Coordinating Board's role is that of coordinating Emmaus Ministries event schedules and sites, training and selecting qualified event leadership, and overseeing the quality of the program. The board leaves the organizing of behind-the-scenes functions of the events to the team leaders (Lay Director, Spiritual Director (in Journey to the Table this position is called Clergy Leader) in cooperation with the local Emmaus Ministries group that is hosting the Emmaus Ministries event. The board decides which ongoing supportive functions the board will care for (literature, kitchen, registration, Team Selection Committee) and which responsibilities the event team leaders and local Emmaus Ministries groups will assume.

In some cases, area-wide or conference-wide Emmaus Communities include several constituent Emmaus Communities in townships within their area that may take responsibility for events at sites nearest them. These area-wide or conference-wide boards may consist of representatives from each of the constituent Communities within the area Emmaus Community. The constituent Communities may elect their own representative(s) to the conference Emmaus Board each year according to a mutually agreed-upon formula. Each constituent Community will then have its own local Emmaus board. Since it takes responsibility for sponsoring Emmaus Ministries events in its locale, the local Emmaus board is best structured as the Working Board described above.

Governing Board

Once a Community hosts or assists with multiple ministries (Walk to Emmaus, Chrysalis, Face to Face, Journey to the Table), the Emmaus Ministries Office recommends that the board take on a Governing Board structure. Managing several ministries and multiple lines of responsibility can become cumbersome. This structure will ensure that each ministry area has the appropriate focus to handle the day-to-day workings, as well as have the needed representation and voice on the board.

* This design will give each Community a Governing Board of ten to sixteen persons, depending on the ministry areas they choose to support.

1. The Governing Board of Directors consists of three classes (size depending on number of ministries managed), a new class being elected each year, with a class rotating off. The Governing Board has three main responsibilities.

a) Handles legalities, including the relationship to The Upper Room Emmaus Ministries Office (Covenant Letter, etc.), finances, insurance, corporate identity, IRS and government paperwork across all ministries.

b) Sets Policies for all ministries to follow.

c) Ensures all ministries operate according to The Upper Room model.

The management of other matters fall under the care of the Ministry Area leadership.

2. The Community or Ministry Areas elect the board by voting each year on nominees selected by a Nominating Committee and approved by the board. These will be position-specific nominations at the discretion of the Nominating Committee. The Governing Board positions are these:

Board Chair

Vice-Chair/Chair-elect

Past Board Chair

Secretary

Treasurer

*Board members representing essential Emmaus Ministries committees
    Team Selection Committee Representative
    Fourth Day Committee Representative
    Agape Committee Representative

*Ministry-Specific positions (as needed as a Community hosts each additional ministry)
    Lay Director and Spiritual Director—Walk to Emmaus
    Lay Director and Spiritual Director—Chrysalis
    Lay Director and Spiritual Director—Face to Face
        Liaison to Journey to the Table

A Liaison to Journey to the Table will only be appointed if the Community *and* the hosting group or organization desires to make use of that support relationship.

The Emmaus Ministries Office suggests that a three (3)-year cycle of electing officers be handled in this way for the Governing Board.

Community-Wide Election

Year 1	Year 2	Year 3
(elect) Vice-Chair	Board Chair	Past Board Chair (Year 2)
Past Board Chair (Year 3)	(elect) Vice-Chair	Board Chair
Board Chair	Past Board Chair (Year 1)	(elect) Vice-Chair
(elect) Secretary	(elect) Treasurer	Agape Chair
Team Selection Chair	Fourth Day Chair	

Ministry Area Election

Year 1	Year 2	Year 3
Walk to Emmaus Lay Director	Walk to Emmaus Spiritual Director	Chrysalis Lay Director
Chrysalis Spiritual Director	Face to Face Lay Director	Face to Face Spiritual Director

The board appoints liaisons to Journey to the Table as necessary.

3. Each specific Ministry Area works in a working or coordinating structure similar to that listed above in the Working or Coordinating Board information with the exception of the Community Spiritual Director position. These duties are carried out by the Ministry Area Spiritual Directors working together as a committee.

4. The *Vice-Chair/Chair-elect* is elected annually for a three-year commitment and gains experience to chair the board the following year. The Past Board Chair offers a voice of experience to the board. This position has voice and vote in all board meetings.

   Ministry Area Spiritual Directors will elect one of their members annually to serve as the designated Community Spiritual Director to the board.

   Team Selection, *Fourth Day*, and *Agape Committee Chairs* work with the Lay Directors and Spiritual Directors to choose members from their specific Ministry Areas to serve on their respective committees.

5. In addition, several other suggested committees could report *to* the board, depending on the need to do so. Each Ministry Area will have members who serve on these committees and the board selects chairs for these committees *from among committee members in each ministry area*. The board may call upon these chairs to report their committees' activities to the Governing Board at meetings. These standing committees include Registration, Outreach, Transportation, Facility and Set-up, Kitchen, Literature/Manuals, Music/Entertainment, Candlelight/Sponsors' Hour, Group Reunions, Gatherings, Communications, and any others deemed necessary. These committees serve many functions, including offering people leadership development opportunities as leaders within the Community. Helpful information about this function can be found in the book *The Board of Directors*.

6. Ministry Areas and committees meet as needed. The Governing Board meetings may be held as often as needed but must meet at least quarterly.

Board members do not serve on Conference Room Teams during their terms on the Board of Directors with the exception of the Board Representative position on each Ministry Area team.

SECTION 3— LEADERSHIP

One of the greatest challenges for every Emmaus Community comes in developing new and mature leaders. A Community member's complaint that "the same people are doing everything" may point to a need for leadership development.

Quite often, the original Emmaus Community or ministry program leaders will continue to carry major responsibility long after the Community or program is well established. Sometimes the original leaders do not want to pass the leadership baton to other people. More often, however, they fear doing so because they believe others do not have an adequate understanding of the Emmaus movement or of its program models.

The development of new leadership in an Emmaus Community requires a desire on the part of the current leaders to cultivate new leaders and to share responsibility. It also demands that the local Emmaus Community place a high priority on the education and training of Community members. When an Emmaus Community intentionally trains its leaders and models adherence to the highest standards, all its ministry programs benefit.

BOARDS AND COMMITTEES

The Covenant Letter between Communities and The Upper Room Emmaus Ministries office emphasizes that each Community is to work to improve its understanding of the Emmaus movement and ensure that each board member receives the necessary training. Pertinent training helps new board members understand their functions and responsibilities, supports continuing board members as they review their responsibilities, and fosters community among the board members.

Leadership development as an ongoing activity occurs within the Emmaus Community's board committees and subcommittees. A description of the board committees can be found in the book *The Board of Directors*. A description of leadership development aspects can be found in the section titled "Why Have Committees?"

Committees are small groups of people who work together for a common goal. (An example of this is the twelve disciples of Jesus.) The optimal size of a committee is three to seven members. Some of the Community's committees will require extra people.

Each chair on the Board of Directors takes responsibility for selecting members from the local Community to serve on his or her committee. Involving members of the Community in the overall work of the board spreads the load and gives everyone a sense of belonging, as well as identifying and training future committee and board leadership. Each committee answers to its chair who then answers to the Board of Directors.

TEAM SELECTION

Team selection guidelines also influence leadership development. Team selection guidelines, agreed upon by the Board of Directors, encourage or require the inclusion of persons who have not yet served in the Conference Room. The guidelines also ensure that a few persons with team experience assume greater responsibility as team leaders, instead of having the Community continue to rely on the same past leaders.

Team Selection Committees are to honor the principle of progressive servanthood as the way of developing spiritual leadership for Emmaus and for the Christian community. Progressive servanthood requires keeping track of people's team experiences and guiding their progression through responsibilities as background servants, Conference Room Team members, and then as mature Christian team leaders.

TEAM FORMATION AND EXPERIENCE

Team experience provides solid educational background for Emmaus Community members. Team meetings not only offer opportunities for learning details about Emmaus and the team's responsibilities on an Emmaus event, but they also prepare members to assume greater responsibility on event teams and in the Emmaus Community in the future.

It behooves team leaders to keep the big picture in mind as they prepare their team members for an Emmaus event. The event team leaders need to plan time in each team meeting to educate other team members about the whys as well as the how-tos of the Emmaus event and its program model. Through well-planned team meetings, team members can grow in their understanding of the Emmaus movement, the rationale behind the event model, the spiritual formation dynamics at the heart of team formation, and the progressive servanthood principle at work in team selection. They also develop a better understanding of the many different persons and committees required to carry out an event. Well led and informative team meetings build future teams and Community leaders.

COMMUNITY GATHERINGS AND TRAINING

Emmaus Community Gatherings are the regular Community-wide meetings. They provide unique opportunities to pass on basic information and education regarding the aim and other aspects of the Emmaus movement. During each meeting, leaders share briefly about one of any number of topics: the responsibilities of sponsors, the selection and formation of teams, the reason behind an aspect of the event experience, the value and format of reunion groups, the spirit of servanthood among team and Community, overview of the various Emmaus ministry programs, and the importance of the church connection. Leaders may include Emmaus education "spots" (brief instructional times) during the opening or closing refreshment time or as part of announcements.

Community Training

Community trainings open leadership development to everyone and help surface new persons for active participation and potential leadership. Each Emmaus Community will plan an annual Community-wide training event, either all-day or half-day Saturday events. Community-wide training events offer many benefits:

- They provide opportunities to gain a greater understanding and appreciation of the pre-event, event, and post-event dimensions of Emmaus.

- They give everyone access to information and instruction on the event models that can otherwise appear to be the possession of a few longtime leaders.

- They serve as refreshers, renewing the Community's vision and zeal for the fruits of the Emmaus event experience and the method of living in grace.

- They help bring forth and identify Community members—both new and old—who exhibit interest and willingness to serve. In other words, training sessions can help identify the *active* Emmaus Community, which is especially helpful in older, established Communities where many people have participated over time.

Training events can provide a basis for opening up the team-selection process and strengthening the leadership base of the Community. A Community can establish team-selection procedures that give preference to persons who take the time and show the commitment to attend annual training sessions. This attendance, combined with good team-selection guidelines, will enrich the team-selection process. Also, a Community may require prospective board members to attend at least one training prior to their nomination. This requirement communicates the importance of training for everyone in the Emmaus Community—new and old members alike. These training sessions need to be widely publicized for team selection or board nomination guidelines to be effective.

Community-wide trainings also improve the quality of sponsored Emmaus events by communicating a common understanding of the purpose of Emmaus and the importance of being trained. Event team leaders are then more accountable to an informed Community and to informed team members for leading the Emmaus events in the proper manner. Teams and the whole Community become more equipped to reflect critically on isolated innovations or changes in the model and can prevent them from developing into traditions for future events.

Training events provide a forum for people to share what they have learned about sponsorship, helping at the event, some aspect of team leadership, or living in the Fourth Day. The entire Community grows in wisdom and knowledge through these opportunities to share learning.

TRAINING HELP FROM THE UPPER ROOM

The Upper Room Emmaus Ministries Office staff, with considerable input and assistance from Regional Leaders and local Communities, has developed a Community Support Structure (CSS). In the CSS, Communicators, Trainers, Consultants, and Start-up Trainers combine efforts to ensure that local Communities are well prepared to receive participants and help them experience God's grace in new and meaningful ways. Each Communicator has the task of building and strengthening the partnership between the Emmaus International Ministries Office and ten to fifteen local Communities. Each Community has a Community-Based Trainer (recruited and trained by The Upper Room) who ensures that the local Community's board and membership remain familiar with and provide the ministry based on The Upper Room model. Consultants are available to Communities that face major challenges. They help nurture local groups back to good health. Start-up Trainers establish and train emerging Communities.

In addition, every other year, Emmaus Ministries Communities receive an invitation to attend regional gatherings where training opportunities are provided.

Finally, in an effort to use available technology, several training modules are available to Community leaders and members online.

This book—*The Upper Room Emmaus Ministries Community Manual*—can also serve as a training manual. Local Emmaus leaders can train other leaders with the assurance that the information in the *Community Manual* agrees with The Upper Room Emmaus Ministries' models.

Other Emmaus Leadership Resources

The availability of official manuals and materials will also encourage and support the development of leadership in the Community. For Emmaus Ministries events, put a copy of the appropriate *Directors' Manual* in the hands of clergy team members in preparation for a time when they may serve as an event Clergy Director (the Journey to the Table program refers to this position as Clergy Leader). To prepare for the team-formation process, team members purchase or receive their copy of the event-specific *Team Manual* for study and discussion. The team leader will also have extra copies of the *Directors' Manual* available for study by prospective team leaders or interested Community members who want to deepen their understanding of the event models. Each person who sits at the Servants' Table (Lay Director, Assistant Lay Directors, Clergy Directors, Music Directors, etc.) also receives a copy of the *Directors' Manual* to prepare for and refer to during the event.

Fourth Day resources (for supporting the spiritual journeys of participants following their Emmaus Ministries events) are also available through The Upper Room. The Upper Room provides a full range of spiritual-life books, magazines, and renewal experiences.

TEAM MEMBER QUALIFICATIONS

(Laity and Clergy)

Qualifications	Why do we have this qualification?	How do we expect these qualifications to be met?	What does this look like?
Servant Leadership	Servant leaders model leadership through service. Jesus led through service and taught his disciples to imitate him and lead in the same manner. Jesus provides us with a model of leadership based on service to God and to others.	Servant leaders are committed to cast vision, set goals, and mobilize others to leave a long-lasting legacy of positive change in the church and in the world.	Servant leadership flows from the leader's character and influences relationships and actions. Servant leaders • invest in people with whom they interact for their long-lasting positive change. • serve and please God and those to whom they are accountable. • recognize that everyone needs love, help, attention, appreciation, and affirmation. • lead through simplicity, humility, compassion, and care. • inspire others to action.
Emmaus Ethos	The Emmaus Ministries have core values that, for best results, must be clear and followed by Community members.	Participate in one of the Emmaus Ministries: Chrysalis, Walk to Emmaus, Journey to the Table, Face to Face, or an recognized Fourth Day Ministry (Tres Dios, Kairos, Cursillo, etc.)	All individuals wishing to serve on an Emmaus Ministries Team shall • agree to submit to the Community Board as they live into their Covenant with Emmaus Ministries and abide by the structure. (Use the outline in preparing talks, abide by time limits, preview talk with team and give same talk on Walk.) • understand that serving in Emmaus Ministries is a privilege not a right.
Accountability Group	All Christians' commitment to a life in grace requires a willingness to be examined and to be supported.	Through devotion to a small group/accountability group that challenges and encourages meaningful contact with Christ through growth in piety, study, and action.	Members of an accountability group offer a life of grace that is seen, among other ways, in the compassion, kindness, humility, gentleness, and patience that characterize their interactions with others.

CLERGY QUALIFICATIONS

Qualifica-tions	Why do we have this qualification?	How do we expect these qualifications to be met?	What does this look like?
Ordination Requirement	In Emmaus Ministries, clergy and laity hold separate roles. However, The Upper Room/ Emmaus does not ordain clergy.	Each denomination, congregation, or church tradition has different requirements to ordain or "license" clergy, which must be examined on an individual basis. The Emmaus Board identifies educational completion, the course of study work, seminars, and other sources of growing in the knowledge of the Bible and God's work when reviewing an application for anyone wishing to serve as clergy in Emmaus Ministries.	The board, under the direction of the Community Spiritual Director, personally examines potential clergy team members and inquires about the following: • By whom and how were they examined and, in their tradition, "licensed" and/or ordained? When did this examination occur? • How does this person evidence engagement in deliberate discipleship (such as seminars, courses of study, college training, etc.)? • Why does this person desire to be a servant in a clergy role in Emmaus Ministries?
Sacramental Authority	Emmaus Spiritual Directors will have many settings in which they will need to serve the sacrament of Holy Communion.	Authorization for the service of Holy Communion is designated by the agency to whom this person is accountable.	The body who has designated this person as "clergy" needs to state parameters of serving the sacrament.
Ministerial Accountability	Persons serving as clergy shall be formally accountable in performing their ministerial roles.	Maintain good standing within ministerial structure and with local Community Emmaus Board	Persons serve in the role of clergy in a manner recognized by the ministerial setting and community in which they serve. • A statement of good standing from an individual's denomination or overseeing authority is submitted to the board. • To ensure the way a clergyperson is serving out the call within the Emmaus Community, he or she is also accountable to the Community Board which has the authority to question, guide, and even dismiss the person from serving within the ministry. If needed, the board may appoint an official mentor to whom the clergy reports and is accountable. This mentor updates the board as necessary.

CLERGY ROLES IN EMMAUS MINISTRIES

	WHY (do we need one)	HOW (they live out their role)	WHAT (they do)	SELECTION
COMMUNITY SPIRITUAL DIRECTOR	A Community, Board, and team need spiritual, theological, moral, and ethical leadership.	**A Spiritual Director accomplishes this as he or she** • assists the Community Board in identifying, developing, and nurturing leaders. • serves as a role model of servant leadership. • assists in selecting those to serve on teams. • coordinates the full participation of clergy in the Community's life.	**Pertaining to the board** • Serves on the board • Is responsible to the board **Pertaining to the Community** • Serves the Community • Models Christ to the Community • Encourages the spiritual health of the Community **Pertaining to other colleagues** • Represents, interprets, promotes the programs to other clergy • Manages the clergy database • Promotes and assists in clergy training **Before the weekend** • Helps select the Weekend Spiritual Director • Ensures theological soundness • Commissions the Conference Room Team **During the Weekend** • Leads pre-Candlelight Communion • Gives hand cross to the Weekend/Event Lay Director • Leads Holy Communion at Closing **Following the Weekend** • Encourages new clergy involvement	**Elected to board by Community** • Annual election • The Board of Directors determines the number of years a clergyperson can serve as Spiritual Director • Progressive servanthood • Elected to the position of Community Spiritual Director by the Board of Directors. • Elected before the regular board elections by the Community • In the case of a Governing Board, the Ministry Area Spiritual Directors elect one of their members to be the Community Spiritual Director.

	WHY (do we need one)	HOW (they live out their role)	WHAT (they do)	SELECTION
EVENT SPIRITUAL DIRECTOR	Teams and participants need spiritual, theological, moral, and ethical leadership.	This person accomplishes this by • partnering with the event lay director in identifying, developing, and nurturing team members and participants. • serving as a role model of servant leadership. • assisting in the team selection and formation process. • coordinating the full participation of clergy in the event.	**Pertaining to the board** • Responsible to the Board **Before the Event** • Helps select Assistant Spiritual Directors • Helps schedule and plan team meetings • Attends all team meetings • Helps prepare the team • Helps prepare Assistant Spiritual Directors for further service **During the Event** • Ensures the theological integrity • Supports the event lay director • Gives MEANS OF GRACE/GOD'S GIFT TO YOU talk • Serves as the pastor at large **Following the Event** • Writes pilgrims' pastors	Community Spiritual Director nominates potential clergy to the Team Selection Committee. Team Selection Committee prioritizes a list of clergy from the registered clergy list and forwards to Community Board for selection. • Is able to maintain theological balance. • Is sensitive to the variety of perspectives in the ecumenical setting. • Demonstrates a team/partnership focus. • Has served at least once for the entire event as an Assistant Spiritual Director under the leadership of an experienced event Spiritual Director. • Has given a minimum of two of the five clergy talks.
EVENT ASSISTANT SPIRITUAL DIRECTOR	To model and develop teamwork and servanthood	Persons accomplish this as they • assist the event Spiritual Director in the clergy duties for the event. • model a servant heart.	• Assist event Spiritual Director • Attends team orientation • Presents assigned talks • Listens to participants after Candlelight • Attends Fourth Day meetings • Prepares for further service	Goes through the Team Selection Process (to ensure progressive servanthood) • Event Spiritual Director develops a list of potential Assistants for Team Selection Committee. • Team Selection Committee completes list of Assistants and forwards it to Community Board for selection. • List goes back to event Spiritual Director who makes calls to assemble team.

SECTION 4—TEAMS

Emmaus Ministries events are led by teams of laypersons and clergypersons. The team guides participants through their event experience and becomes, for the participants, a community of Christian love in which they can experience God's transforming grace.

The steps involved in building a team include the following:

- selecting the team members,
- helping them learn their various roles and responsibilities, and
- growing together spiritually and functionally through a series of team meetings.

TEAM LEADER SELECTION

The Community Board or Steering Committee, as part of the covenant with The Upper Room, is responsible for selecting quality team leaders for the events. Only a recognized Emmaus Ministries Community may offer Walk to Emmaus, Chrysalis, and Face to Face events. For each of these ministries, the board will select a Lay Director and a Spiritual Director (Journey to the Table refers to this position as Clergy Leader), and for Face to Face a Logistics Leader.

An Emmaus Ministries Community or other organizations, such as a campus ministry or chaplain's office in covenant with The Upper Room, may offer Journey to the Table. For these latter instances, the covenanting organization may have a core leadership group select the top leadership positions for the Journey to the Table event. For any Journey to the Table event, the selected top leaders will include a Team Leader and a Spiritual Leader. If both of these leaders are above the age of participants on the Journey to the Table event, a third position is necessary: the Peer Leader. The Peer Leader works alongside the Team Leader and falls within the age group of young adult participants.

The board finalizes the selection of the events leaders *at least one year prior* to the planned event. Some Community Boards choose their event leaders even farther in advance so they will have a chance to watch closely and learn from the leaders of other events. Each event, whether offered separately or simultaneously with another, requires its own event leaders.

In most Communities, the selection of event team leaders is part of an ongoing board conversation about emerging leadership and the most qualified candidates for the position. The Community Spiritual Director guides the recommendation of the event's clergy team leader.

The Community Spiritual Director is encouraged to bring recommendations to the board a year or more in advance. This timing allows qualified clergy to free their schedules for those events.

Selection of the event team leaders is a matter of discernment through prayer and consensus of the Community Board.

Qualifications and Expectations for the Team Leaders

The lay team leader for the event leads a team through team formation and the team and participants through an event. The lay team leader is the principal layperson who directs activities during the Emmaus event. For Walk to Emmaus, Chrysalis, and Face to Face, a layperson fills this position. For Journey to the Table, this position can be filled with either a layperson or clergyperson.

The board selects the event lay team leader on the basis of spiritual and technical readiness for the role of forming a team and acting as the public leader of the event. It helps for the person to have the gifts and disposition to lead people and to coordinate the multiple aspects of planning an Emmaus Ministries event. The event lay team leader commits to leading the event according to The Upper Room model and under the authority of the Community Board. The event lay team leader commits the time to plan and lead the team meetings, to tend to many details, and to work cooperatively with the event clergy team leader. This person needs to be participating in an ongoing faith-based community and meeting with a small group of Christians for consistent support.

Additionally, for Walk to Emmaus and Face to Face, the Lay Director's experience would include serving on Emmaus Ministries events in the background and on teams in a variety of positions. This team involvement will include having served multiple times as an assistant lay team leader and as a Table Leader.

The event clergy team leader is the primary Spiritual Director of the event. The role requires sufficient experience and training for this job. (See Clergy Role Qualifications in Section 3.)

An event clergy team leader must be capable of giving the clergy team leader's talk, show evidence of spiritual maturity as a person in active ministry, and have an understanding of the nature and purpose of the Emmaus movement in relation to the church. Event clergy team leaders actively support the Emmaus movement and practice the Emmaus model (piety, study, and action). The event clergy team leader should be authorized to administer the sacrament of Holy Communion in a manner consistent with the custom of Emmaus. The event clergy team leader, like the lay team leader, must commit to participate in all the preparatory team meetings and the entire event.

Alongside the event lay team leader, the clergy team leader is responsible for the proper preparation of the team and for conducting the event according to The Upper Room Emmaus Ministries model. While team leaders work as partners in leadership, the event clergy team leader plays a support role in relation to the lay team leader in team formation and during the event, emphasizing the importance of lay leadership through Emmaus.

The clergy team leader serves as pastor-at-large for the team during team formation and for the participants during the Emmaus event, working with the event lay team leader to ensure that the process of team formation and talk preparation equips and spiritually enriches team members. The event clergy team leader also exercises special care for the theological integrity of the talks during team formation and during the event.

Ideally, an event clergy team leader has given all the clergy talks on previous events (with the possible exception of the one talk preassigned to the event clergy team leader). At a minimum, however, the event clergy team leader will have served an entire event in residence on an Emmaus team as an event assistant team leader at least once under the leadership of an experienced event clergy team leader. Beyond this, Communities set standards of their own for the further preparation of their event clergy team leaders.

In the book *Spiritual Directors,* the author emphasizes two significant points: (1) the event clergy team leader is available during the Emmaus event "for holy listening," and (2) "the intention of spiritual direction is to engage an individual in conversation about God's presence and calling in his or her life."

TEAM MEMBER SELECTION

(See "Team Member Qualifications" in Section 3.) Once the board has selected the event team leaders, the selection process for the remainder of the team begins. The goal is to begin this selection process at least *six months prior* to the event.

Team Selection Committee refers to the group responsible for selecting the remaining team members for an Emmaus Ministries event. That may refer to a standing committee with a board member serving as the committee chair or a smaller group serving as needed. The Team Selection Committee also helps assign the talks for the event.

For an Emmaus Ministries Community, the Community Board or Steering Committee establishes the Team Selection Committee:

- a board or Steering Committee member who is responsible for team selection and who serves as committee chairperson,
- event team leaders,
- two to four members of the Community (nonboard members) who represent a cross-section of the Community, including at least one youth for a Chrysalis event or one young adult for Journey to the Table, all of whom have a broad awareness of the Community membership and a solid understanding of team needs.

The Community Spiritual Director works with the Team Selection Committee to provide continuity for the long-range selection of clergy and cultivation of a pool of future event spiritual leaders.

The Team Selection Committee helps achieve the stated goals for the team selection process:

- *Choosing strong and balanced teams.*

  The Team Selection Committee provides a broader awareness of prospective team members and their gifts. This awareness helps the team selection process move beyond the limited circle of the team leaders' friends and acquaintances. The committee can more fully consider the experience and gifts of people the team needs.

- *Achieving broad involvement of the Community.*

  Over time, the Team Selection Committee can strive to involve as many willing and able members of the Community as possible, for their good and for the health of the Community. An event lay team leader may only have in mind the goal of forming one team for one event; the Team Selection Committee concerns itself with both the building of the team and the building of the entire Community into a body of mature, Christian leaders.

- *Cultivating new leadership.*

  By following established team selection guidelines, the Team Selection Committee provides continuity in the selection process from event to event. A Team Selection Committee can, therefore, intentionally develop new leaders by encouraging people to move through team roles with increasing leadership over the course of several events.

- *Helping team members grow in grace as servant leaders.*

  The Team Selection Committee serves as an avenue of corporate discernment for the Community. In this capacity, the Team Selection Committee provides a method of growing Christian leadership in individuals. By involving new leaders, inviting individuals to roles of increasing leadership, and facilitating ongoing conversation about the gifts and graces of each individual, the Team Selection Committee plays an important role in ongoing Christian discipleship.

TEAM SELECTION RESPONSIBILITIES

Once the Team Selection Committee chair has been notified of the confirmed selections of the event team leaders, he/she sets a date with them to meet for team selection—no later than four (4) months before the date of the event and then notifies committee members of the time and place of the meeting. The Team Selection Committee begins praying for guidance in the team selection process. The Team Selection Committee chair ensures that the event team leaders receive The Upper Room and Community-developed materials needed for their roles (such as the *Directors' Manual*, key role checklists, talk outlines, a sample "welcome to the team" letter with team meeting dates, team meeting notes, or handouts).

Prior to the team selection meeting, the chair and others on the Team Selection Committee gather names of potential team members. Committee members may obtain names from Community membership records that indicate persons' previous team experience, their active support of previous events (such as the prayer vigil, meal preparation or snack agape, facility setup and cleanup), and their participation in available training programs. Names of potential team members also may be submitted to the Team Selection Committee throughout the year. In addition to having event participants fill out volunteer sheets at the end of their event, the event's team members may present names of event participants whom they feel would be good team members in the future.

The Team Selection Committee attempts to secure broad representation of the Community as it develops its list of potential team members. The Emmaus Community leadership and the Team Selection Committee share the responsibility for determining a young person's readiness to serve as an adult on an event team. The decision to ask a young person to serve as an adult leader is one to make carefully and prayerfully, based on the characteristics expected of all adult leaders regardless of age. The Team Selection Committee will look for demonstrated leadership skills within his or her faith community, the young person's place of employment, and the wider community.

For each position on a team, the committee selects a person and lists one or two more persons as backup. The event team leaders may come to the meeting prepared to make recommendations to the committee, or they may rely solely on the committee's suggestions. However, the selection process is based on prayer and spiritual discernment, not on personal preferences or need for recognition. The Community Spiritual Director works closely with the event clergy team leader and the Team Selection Committee in selecting clergy for the teams.

After the board approves the Team Selection Committee list(s), the event team leaders begin calling their prospective team members. If several prospective team members and their backups cannot serve, then the event team leader contacts the Team Selection Committee to discuss additional names.

When the team has been confirmed, the event lay team leader sends the team roster to the Team Selection Committee chair and to the communications team for publication.

TEAM SELECTION GUIDELINES

Qualifications and expectations for each team member role are listed below. Where the roles are similar between Emmaus ministries, the information relies on a single description. More detailed information is available in each of the Emmaus Ministries *Directors' Manual* and *Team Manual*. Also see "Team and Clergy Role Qualifications" in Section 3.

The Background Leader / Background Teams / Support Leaders / Event Support team roles are the silent servants who become the "hands and feet" of each event. These roles include those on the kitchen team, agape team, Prayer Chapel team, and logistics team. The importance of their positions and work cannot be overstated: They are servants who make sure that things run smoothly and that people have what they need at the right time. Most of all, they make it possible for the Conference Room Team to remain focused on the event and the Holy Spirit's work within each person.

The Assistant Table Leader / Table Leader / Youth Table Leader / Adult Table Leader roles require persons who can listen and empathize, guide discussion, and foster the development of the table families. The participants experience most of the event and develop lasting relationships at the table. The Table Leaders facilitate table interaction in response to each talk and support the building of *koinonia*, Christian community, among those at the table. The various Table Leader assignments are made with care and given to people who have a proven ability to lead a group, whether in a previous Emmaus Ministries event or another faith-based group.

The Assistant Music Leader / Music Leader roles are responsible for planning and leading the music during team formation and the Emmaus Ministries event. Music leadership is a ministry that calls for prayer, preparation, and flexibility. Music leaders do not have to be professionally trained and have impressive voices. The preferred gifts for music leaders include skill and a servant spirit, sensitivity to the moods and needs of the event participants, and readiness to lead with energy and joy at any moment. The music leaders draw people closer to God and to one another through music. They work cooperatively with the event team leaders. Music leaders are the same gender as the event participants.

The Media Leader role provides the audiovisual support for the event in the conference room and other spaces. Because the Media Leader works with the talk presenters, it helps if he or she has prior team experience. The role requires training or experience in the use of sound and projection equipment and software.

The Board Representative role does not provide leadership in the team process unless his or her counsel is sought. The Board Representative functions only in a support role among the team members. The Board Representative is available to the event team leaders before the event to answer questions and give direction when asked. He or she participates in all team meetings. The Board Representative can be any board member of the same gender as the event participants—except the Community Lay Director. If no one on the board is available, the board may appoint a recent past board member or past event lay team leader to serve in this role for the event.

For Journey to the Table, this position emphasizes a valuable mentorship role to the event team leaders. The rapid turnover in young adult leaders makes an experienced mentor available throughout the process invaluable.

The Assistant Lay Director / Coach / Assistant Team Leader roles help the event lay team leader prepare the team prior to the event and make sure the event itself runs smoothly and on schedule. They free the event lay team leader of concern for details as much as possible so he or she can pay attention to the team, participants, and overall progress of the event. They serve as the timekeepers for the event and anticipate preparation for each aspect of the event.

For Walk to Emmaus, Chrysalis, and Face to Face, these persons have been Table Leaders and given talks on previous Emmaus Ministries events.

The Assistant Spiritual Leader role assists the event clergy team leader when called upon and serves as a spiritual guide to the event participants. Each prepares a talk for the event.

Honoring Emmaus Community Participation

The Team Selection Committee regards participation in an accountable spiritual support group (group reunions or Next Steps groups) and Community Gatherings as a sign of a person's commitment to the Community. While ideally all team members would be active in their specific Walk to Emmaus Reunion Group, Chrysalis Next Steps group, etc., the event lay team leader and a person giving the Fourth Day (Walk to Emmaus) or Next Steps (Chrysalis) talk can only bear authentic witness if they are involved in such a group. Above all, the committee discerns individual gifts for team membership and overall commitment to the aims of Emmaus Ministries.

Anonymous Positions of Servanthood

Emmaus leadership begins and ends with anonymous positions of servanthood, such as participating in the prayer vigil, contributing agape items, or praying in the chapel. This kind of sacrifice and servanthood is the heart of Emmaus Ministries and the place where the development of Christian leadership begins. Those who first give themselves wholeheartedly and joyfully to the humblest duties may eventually be with the participants in the conference room, setting an example and sharing their lives and spirit.

Progressive Servanthood

The design of Emmaus Ministries team structure fosters a progression of responsibility and an increasing level of leadership for each individual. When selecting individuals for team positions, the committee carefully considers each person's leadership experience and the leadership experience of the team as a whole. When done well, this process will ensure that all team members build their experience and gain new leadership abilities.

This attitude of progressive servanthood is balanced with the specific gifts and preparedness of an individual to determine where he or she is best suited to serve. An individual who speaks well publicly may be well-suited to speak during the event but may not yet have the organizational abilities to move up to an event team leader position. Such an individual receives the opportunity to develop his or her organizational abilities while also using the gift of speaking. Conversely, an individual who has only served as a music leader but who has speaking or organizational abilities need not be constrained to serving only in a music role. Many positions benefit greatly from specific gifts and abilities, but all individuals may have an opportunity to serve in a progression of responsibilities as they grow.

In the team selection process, the committee keeps in mind that the focus of progressive servanthood is on persons' spiritual formation rather than the position they fill. People can experience great spiritual maturation and never serve on an event team—a great gain to the body of Christ. Conversely, people who serve in multiple roles of increasing responsibility on an event team but move no farther along on their spiritual journey will have missed the more important opportunity. Event leaders pay close attention to their own spiritual journey and empower others to do the same. After all, Emmaus Ministries exists to empower leaders to be the hands and feet of Christ, regardless of the team positions they fill.

The table below lists the team role progressions for Walk to Emmaus and Face to Face. The number in parentheses after the team role name indicates the number serving in that role. Clergy leadership progression involves serving as an Assistant Spiritual Director in a resident role at least twice. Then the clergyperson can be considered for the clergy event leader role. In the table that follows

* indicates the role is the *Assistant Lay Event Leader* for the listed event;

** indicates the role is the *Lay Event Leader* for the listed event.

Event	Prog.	Team Role	Eligibility Criteria
Walk to Emmaus	1	Event Support (multiple)	served in support on previous events
Walk to Emmaus	2	Assistant Table Leader (1 per table)	served in support on previous events
Walk to Emmaus	2	Assistant Music Leader	served in support on previous events
Walk to Emmaus	3	Table Leader (1 per table)	served as Assistant Table Leader
Walk to Emmaus	3	Music Leader	sufficient team experience to understand role of music for event; served as Assistant Music Leader
Walk to Emmaus	4	* Assistant Lay Director (3)	served as Table Leader
Walk to Emmaus	4	Board Representative	member of the Emmaus board or a previous board member or Lay Director
Walk to Emmaus	5	** Lay Director	served twice as Assistant Lay Director

Event	Prog.	Team Role	Eligibility Criteria
Face to Face	1	Support Assistant (multiple)	served in support on previous events
Face to Face	2	Support Leader (Agape, Kitchen, Prayer Team, Logistics)	served in support on previous events
Face to Face	2	Table Leader (1 per table)	served in support on previous events
Face to Face	2	Music Leader	served in support on previous events
Face to Face	2	Media Leader	served in support on previous events
Face to Face	3	*Coaches (2)	1 male and 1 female; served as Table Leader or as Walk to Emmaus Assistant Lay Director or Board Representative
Face to Face	3	Board Representative	member of the Emmaus board or previous board member or Lay Director
Face to Face	4	** Lay Director	served as a Coach or as Walk to Emmaus Lay Director

- For Chrysalis and Journey to the Table, the Team Selection Committee evaluates the relevant experience, gifts, graces, and spiritual growth of each prospective team member. That evaluation would include experience in Emmaus Ministries events as well as experience and leadership in other ministries and aspects of life. Progressive servanthood offers the same benefits in these ministries with young people. The Team Selection Committee for these two programs realize that younger leaders will move through the age group of these ministries more quickly. A well-balanced team might have one-third of its team members serving for the first time, one-third have served in comparable leadership roles at least once before, and one-third who have extensive leadership in ministries.

Talk Assignments

The Team Selection Committee makes the talk assignments. The progression of talk assignments for team members varies from Community to Community. Some Communities follow a specific order, slowly moving both lay and clergy team members through the talks occurring early in the event to those occurring near the end of the event. Other Communities only consider the number and variety of talks a team member has given. Still others reserve particular lay talks for the most experienced Emmaus Ministries team members.

The committee assigns team members topics that they can communicate with insight and experience whether they are new or seasoned team members.

The table below includes notes to aid in the assignment of talks to the selected team members. For each Emmaus ministry, several talks are preassigned to a specific team role; those are indicated in the Assignment Notes column of the table.

More detailed information is available in each of the Emmaus ministries' *Directors' Manual* and *Team Manual*.

Event	Talk Name	Assignment Notes
Walk to Emmaus	PRIORITY	Assistant Lay Director
Walk to Emmaus	PREVENIENT GRACE	Assistant Spiritual Director
Walk to Emmaus	PRIESTHOOD OF ALL BELIEVERS	Table Leader (or assistant Table Leader)
Walk to Emmaus	JUSTIFYING GRACE	Assistant Spiritual Director
Walk to Emmaus	LIFE OF PIETY	Table Leader; talk summarizes fundamental concepts in the Emmaus message
Walk to Emmaus	GROW THROUGH STUDY	Table Leader (or assistant Table Leader)
Walk to Emmaus	MEANS OF GRACE	Spiritual Director; ensures talk (and Dying Moments) is led by one with the experience and ability to handle with grace and clarity
Walk to Emmaus	CHRISTIAN ACTION	Table Leader (or assistant Table Leader)
Walk to Emmaus	OBSTACLES TO GRACE	Assistant Spiritual Director
Walk to Emmaus	DISCIPLESHIP	Table Leader; talk summarizes fundamental concepts in the Emmaus message
Walk to Emmaus	CHANGING OUR WORLD	Table Leader; talk focuses on the Fourth Day aim to be the church in the world
Walk to Emmaus	SANCTIFYING GRACE	Assistant Spiritual Director
Walk to Emmaus	BODY OF CHRIST	Table Leader; talk focuses on the Fourth Day aim to be the church in the world

Walk to Emmaus	PERSEVERANCE	Lay Director; has sacrificed and persevered as the event leader; possesses spiritual maturity and embodies the Emmaus method for living
Walk to Emmaus	FOURTH DAY	Assistant Lay Director (preserves integrity of table groups); must have an informed and authentic enthusiasm for Fourth Day activities
Event	**TALK NAME**	**Assignment Notes**
Chrysalis	IDEALS	Youth team member; one who understands the event flow to ensure it is properly launched (ideals theme underlies the entire event)
Chrysalis	GOD DESIGNED YOU	Assistant Spiritual Leader
Chrysalis	FAITH	Adult team member
Chrysalis	GOD LOVES YOU	Assistant Spiritual Director
Chrysalis	PRODIGAL	Youth team member
Chrysalis	COMMUNICATION THROUGH PRAYER	Adult team member
Chrysalis	CHRISTIAN GROWTH THROUGH STUDY	Youth team member
Chrysalis	GOD'S GIFT TO YOU	Spiritual Director; ensures talk (and Holy Communion) are led by one with the experience and ability to handle with grace and clarity
Chrysalis	MARRIAGE	(married) Adult team member
Chrysalis	GOD SUSTAINS YOU	Assistant Spiritual Director
Chrysalis	CHRISTIAN ACTION	Youth team member
Chrysalis	SINGLE LIFE	(single) Adult team member
Chrysalis	GOD EMPOWERS YOU	Assistant Spiritual Director
Chrysalis	PRIESTHOOD OF ALL BELIEVERS	Lay Director; has persevered as the event leader; has credibility to summarize the three days around the theme of God's call
Chrysalis	NEXT STEPS	Youth Assistant Lay Director
Event	**TALK NAME**	**Assignment Notes**
Face to Face	PRIORITY	Lay Director
Face to Face	PREVENIENT GRACE	Assistant Spiritual Director
Face to Face	PRIESTHOOD OF ALL BELIEVERS	Table Leader (or assistant Table Leader)
Face to Face	JUSTIFYING GRACE	Assistant Spiritual Director
Face to Face	LIFE OF PIETY	Table Leader (or assistant Table Leader)
Face to Face	MEANS OF GRACE	Spiritual Director
Face to Face	CHRISTIAN ACTION	Table Leader (or assistant Table Leader)
Face to Face	OBSTACLES TO GRACE	Assistant Spiritual Director
Face to Face	DISCIPLESHIP	Table Leader (or assistant Table Leader)

Face to Face	CHANGING OUR WORLD	Table Leader (or assistant Table Leader)
Face to Face	SANCTIFYING GRACE	Assistant Spiritual Director
Face to Face	BODY OF CHRIST	Table Leader (or assistant Table Leader)
Face to Face	COPING IN TOUGH TIMES	Hospice speaker or someone who has lost a spouse; person may be either lay or clergy and need not have attended Emmaus event
Face to Face	PERSEVERANCE IN THE NEXT DAY	Lay Director
Event	**TALK NAME**	**Assignment Notes**
Journey to the Table	IDENTITY, PART ONE—WHO WE ARE	
Journey to the Table	IDENTITY, PART TWO—WHOSE WE ARE	Spiritual Leader or Assistant
Journey to the Table	BALANCING LIFE	
Journey to the Table	STUDYING AND GROWTH	
Journey to the Table	RELATIONSHIPS WITH GOD AND OTHERS	
Journey to the Table	A LOVE THAT STRENGTHENS	Spiritual Leader or Assistant
Journey to the Table	PRIESTHOOD OF ALL BELIEVERS	Spiritual Leader or Assistant
Journey to the Table	CHRISTIAN ACTION	
Journey to the Table	PERSEVERANCE AND COMMITMENT	Assistant Team Leader
Journey to the Table	MAKE A SPACE	Team Leader or Peer Leader

The One-Third Rule

A goal of the Team Selection Committee is to staff each team with approximately one-third (1) new Conference Room Team members, (2) second-time or third-time team members, and (3) team veterans. Veterans provide continuity and confidence, while newer members bring fresh energy and enthusiasm. This guideline helps a Community integrate fresh faces on the team and expands the Community's leadership base. Each Emmaus Ministries event becomes an opportunity to incorporate new persons into teams and to move those with some experience gradually into other leadership positions.

Clergy Involvement as Leaders

The Team Selection Committee strives to include on each team a clergyperson who shows promise as a future event team leader. In this way, those who meet the guidelines to be an event team leader receive regular training and preparation to serve as one by experiencing the entire event from the team side. The Team Selection Committee also tries to include on each team a clergyperson who has never served as a team member. This approach to selection helps the Community expand the pool of potential event clergy team leaders and deepens clergy appreciation for the Emmaus ministry through their involvement. The Team Selection Committee plans ahead with the sponsoring organization's spiritual leader and asks clergy twelve months in advance to commit to an entire Emmaus Ministries event. The payoff in clergy support is worth the effort.

Lay Involvement as Leaders

The Team Selection Committee will wisely select at least one event assistant lay team leader who is experienced and confident in this role and at least one who is new to the job. This choice gives the event lay team leader and team confidence that the assistants' work will be accomplished with competence but also trains new assistants for future teams.

Theological Balance

The Team Selection Committee strives for a sound balance of theological orientations and religious styles on teams. Team members may reflect a diverse set of Christian perspectives, but they must also create an atmosphere of openness and unity for all participants. Teams dominated by any one Christian perspective or denomination do not represent the diversity and unity of the church universal.

Male and Female Clergy on Teams

Team Selection Committees intentionally recruit both men and women clergy among the clergy speakers on teams for both men's and women's events. This rationale represents the reality of pastoral leadership for both men and women in the church universal today. The Office recommends that the Spiritual Director be the same gender as participants.

Male and Female Laypersons on Teams

In the Face to Face experience, men and women participate together. In a Journey to the Table experience, participants may be both genders or the hosting organization may offer the event as a separate male and female experience. The team selection for these two ministries would reflect the desired audience of participants. For Face to Face and for a joint offering of Journey to the Table, the team would have a balance of male and female team members. For separate gender events, the lay team members for each experience should be the same gender as the participants.

Grace Talks by Clergy

The concept of grace is the centerpiece of the Emmaus Ministries event; the clergy talks provide the background of grace before which the event's message unfolds. These talks are given by those trained by the church in word and sacrament so as to communicate a proper understanding of grace.

Involvement of Many Clergy

An event team has many clergy members, which offers several advantages:

- Many share the workload of the numerous talks and spiritual responsibilities. Each clergy member typically takes time to prepare one talk well and is then free to give attention to the participants.

- Participants hear the message of grace from the perspective and experience of many different clergy.

- More clergy can be involved in the Community and trained more quickly, since not all are required to stay for the entire event. This expands the pool of available and experienced clergy for future teams.

For Walk to Emmaus and Face to Face, at least two clergy remain in residence for the entire event: the Spiritual Director and one Assistant Spiritual Director.

For Chrysalis and Journey to the Table, the Spiritual Director remains in residence for the entire event.

The other assistants present one talk and are encouraged to remain for as much of the event as possible. The Spiritual Director may ask one or more assistants to help with the event's clergy meditations and Communion, and other times as needed.

Lay Table Leaders

Assigning laypersons to the Table Leader roles gives them the opportunity to grow as small-group leaders. Sometimes, a clergy leader could inhibit group discussion among laypersons who view clergy as authorities with all the answers. The largely lay leadership of an event makes a statement to the participants about the commitment, gifts, and leadership potential of church laity.

TEAM FORMATION

Team members become a genuine team through an intentional period of team formation. Team formation occurs during a series of well-planned team meetings that involve both lay and clergy team members. Throughout the process, team members prepare and grow together to become God's hands and feet during the event.

Reasons for Team Formation

An intentional team formation process is essential to fulfilling the goals of the Emmaus Ministries movement:

1. *To prepare team members functionally.* Through team meetings, all team members prepare themselves for their responsibilities on the event. Rehearsing talks and responsibilities during team meetings releases anxiety. Practicing also reassures team members that God is indeed present and will be powerfully present on the event. Furthermore, team

members have a chance to work through their own responses to talks ahead of time so they can be more attentive to the participants' responses during the event.

2. *To prepare team members spiritually.* The event team leaders attempt to make each person's experience on the team a spiritual exercise and an opportunity for spiritual growth. For example, each talk gives its presenter an opportunity to grow both in understanding and in practicing the topic of the talk. Team meetings offer occasions to encourage team members to put their spiritual lives in order, to remember who and whose they are, and to reflect upon God's call to this ministry. The meetings foster the renewal of the practices of piety, study, and action.

3. *To build a spirit of Christian community.* The leadership for these events is not a group of individuals carrying out assigned tasks but a *team* of people who are becoming a Christian community. This Community provides the caring environment in which the participants come to live for a time. Each aspect of team meetings—worship, sharing, team education, talk previews, prayer—works toward providing a bonding experience for team members. The team moves from being strangers to being friends in Christ: people who know and care about one another, who appreciate one another's strengths and weaknesses. The event team leaders' most significant work is the preparation and building of the team.

4. *To train leaders for future events.* Team formation is a primary way people learn about Emmaus Ministries events and how they are led. Through the hands-on experience of team meetings, the team leaders pass on the common wisdom of the Emmaus movement to newer members of the Community and cultivate new leaders. If the team leaders neglect team formation, the Community will never develop new leaders who are well-grounded in the purpose and procedures of the movement.

5. *To develop Christian leaders for work outside the Community.* The importance of team formation resides in the Community's purpose beyond simply carrying out events: the development of Christian maturity and leadership. Team participation helps form individuals as Christians and as spiritual leaders. Team members cultivate the practical and spiritual skills to become Christian leaders in their church and Community. Members exercise their individual gifts during team meetings and focus their energies on service to God. They learn to articulate their faith through talk preparation; pray together and intercede for others; gently lead a group in discussing deep and sensitive subjects; maintain a humble, servant attitude; live in community; work as a team; actively listen to people; and pay attention to God's presence in the midst of human interaction.

Orientation Session

The first step toward team formation is a team orientation session. Community leadership organizes and presents an orientation session prior to the first team meeting. The orientation session includes all Conference Room Team members and all support team members. The orientation session details the roles and responsibilities of each team participant. It includes information about the cloistered nature of the conference room and the role of anonymous servanthood for the support staff. People not serving on the upcoming event conduct the orientation session.

Team Meetings

It is essential that team members participate in the entire team process. Those contacting prospective team members tell them of the expected commitment. In many Communities, a general rule of thumb is that team members participate in at least three-fourths of the total number of team meetings. Many active persons have difficulty scheduling around family, school, work, and church obligations. Nevertheless, the formation of a team requires that team members commit time to team meetings.

Clergy team members are expected to participate in team meetings as well. The Spiritual Director sets the example by committing to attend all team meetings and previewing the talks. The team needs to build rapport with the clergy, and all team members will benefit from their spiritual guidance before the event.

For Walk to Emmaus, Chrysalis, and Face to Face, team meetings involve only the Conference Room Team: those who will actually be in the conference room with the participants for the entire event. Though support persons working behind the scenes are an integral part of the event, team meeting attendance will not directly help them perform their duties. Involving support persons in team meetings may unnecessarily overextend these servants.

For Journey to the Table team meetings include all team members, including the Background Leaders. The Background Leaders' knowledge of the event will help them coordinate the work of remote volunteers who may know nothing about the schedule or event.

Team meetings generally consist of several elements:

- **Worshiping together** at the beginning of each meeting. Lay and clergy team members can rotate leadership for this time of worship or Communion.

- **Sharing our spiritual lives** in "floating" group reunions. For a few minutes after worship, the event lay team leader may invite participants to gather in groups of two or three to respond to a question or two from the group reunion card or other questions the event team leaders choose. This sharing fosters team relationships, focuses the team on the spiritual life, and readies the team inwardly for the remainder of the meeting.

- **Developing a thorough understanding of Emmaus.** For a few minutes at each meeting, an event team leader expands team members' understanding of the ministry by reviewing one aspect of the program and the team's responsibilities. The *Team Manual* may be used for this purpose, with the team reading an assigned portion that is then reviewed at the subsequent meeting.

- **Helping one another prepare** for and practice the tasks: talk previews, table leadership, and music leadership.

- **Praying together** at the close of the meeting and throughout team formation. Prayer undergirds and empowers each event from beginning to end, including the prayers of the team throughout team formation. Praying for one another extends God's love to another and binds the team together as a family of God. In addition to taking time at each meeting to pray corporately, each team member is assigned a prayer partner for whom he or she prays through the duration of team formation.

Team meetings are not the place to work out details of buying food, organizing food or acts of agape, deciding whom to assign for this or that, and so on. These responsibilities belong to specific persons who do their work outside of team meetings. The event lay team leader and the assistants will meet separately from team meetings to ensure that support needs are being handled. Good planning and wise use of team meeting time fosters positive team morale and confidence in the team leaders.

Furthermore, team meetings do not *only* consist of a series of tasks for completion so everyone can get home. The primary purpose of team meetings is building the team. Even when assignments and tasks are completed and meetings wrap up early, the event lay team leader will make use of the remaining time to build relationships, skills, and a servant attitude.

Previewing Talks

All speakers—lay and clergy alike—present their talk to the team just as they will present the talk at the event. This gives the speakers the chance to practice the talk and gain strength from the team's affirmation and suggestions for improvements. No one is above improvement, and the team offers suggestions in an atmosphere of care and affirmation. Previewing the talks underscores the fact that each speaker depends upon the others to convey the total message of the event. When a team member presents a talk and receives the team's comments, the talk no longer belongs just to that speaker but to the entire team. The event clergy team leader takes an active role in talk previews to ensure theological soundness, clarity, and relevance to real life. The Spiritual Director meets with those experiencing difficulty in pulling their talks together.

Many Communities have the tradition of all speakers wearing semiformal clothing, such as suits or dresses, when giving a talk. "Special" items should not be worn, other than the speaker's Emmaus cross, that would separate or distinguish the speaker from others. For clergy, this includes robes or vestments.

Preparing Table Leaders

The Table Leader holds the most influential job in the conference room. A Table Leader can make all the difference in a person's experience of the event, for better or for worse. So Table Leaders deserve sufficient orientation and training for their role.

- Talk preview discussions in small groups during team meetings can provide the opportunity for team members to practice guiding a small-group discussion.

- A well-planned team discussion on the role of the Table Leader and on keys to effective table leadership can elicit a wealth of insight from team members on helpful table leadership.

- A Table Leader training workshop that includes presentation, discussion, and role play held during a team meeting can be a valuable tool.
- For each Emmaus ministry program, the *Directors' Manual* and *Team Manual* contain information and handouts about table leadership and the Table Leader's responsibilities.

Preparing Music Leaders

Music Leaders can prepare themselves and the team by leading music during team meetings and teaching the members songs necessary to the event. Worship times during team meetings offer the occasions to try out special music for the event. A brief discussion on team members' experiences of good music leadership can encourage and strengthen the Music Leaders. The event team leaders meet with the Music Leaders to make sure they share common expectations for the Music Leaders roles during the event and to plan for music on the event.

Fostering Team Spirit

Team spirit goes far beyond a sense of camaraderie, enthusiasm, or closeness. It embodies a servant attitude, a willingness to take a back seat to the participants, and a readiness to set aside team member differences in doctrine and opinion for the sake of unity in the love of Christ.

In Galatians 5:22-26, the apostle Paul lists "the fruit of the Spirit," characteristics of the Holy Spirit manifested in people's attitudes and behavior. This fruit represents the character of a team properly formed in the spirit of Jesus Christ. Emmaus Ministries wants participants to feast on this fruit throughout their event. The fruit of the Spirit serves as a good backdrop for describing team attitudes and practices. Team leaders can use the fruit of the Spirit as a basis for sharing and reflecting in preparation for the event.

Developing Team Meeting Schedules

Team-formation schedules need to include enough hours to preview all the talks and build the team. This number derives from the various elements to be accomplished: worship, group reunions and team building, training on specific topics, talk previews, and prayer time. Each Community works out a schedule that best suits its situation in order to fulfill the goals of team formation. For a full-length Walk to Emmaus or Chrysalis event, one of the following schedules may be useful. For Journey to the Table events, which have fewer talks to preview, the team may decide to spend more time building community with one another or have fewer total hours of team meetings.

- *Eight to ten weekly meetings.* This schedule employs weekly meetings of approximately three hours each. This plan especially suits Communities in which team members live, work, or attend school close enough to one another to make weekly evening meetings possible. An extended number of meetings gives the team time to grow together gradually. This schedule also gives the event team leaders plenty of time to notice and respond to needs among the team members.

- *Four biweekly or monthly meetings.* This schedule consists of four all-day meetings of about six hours each. This schedule especially suits Communities in which team members must drive long distances to meetings, which makes successive weekly and evening meetings difficult. This schedule requires four talk previews for each meeting (one meeting will have three talk previews. Seasoned team members can preview their talks at the first meeting to serve as a model for new team members. Other than requiring the preview of more talks at each meeting, the elements of each session follow the description above.

- *Two Friday evening and all-day Saturday meetings.* This schedule consists of two meetings each starting on Friday evening and ending on Saturday evening (meeting hours would be roughly 7 p.m.–10 p.m. on Friday, and 9 a.m.–5 p.m. on Saturday, an option that often works well for Chrysalis Team Meetings). Each meeting may require that some team members spend the night. The team members living close enough to go home Friday night could graciously host those who cannot return home overnight. This schedule again provides all the elements of the team meetings. To make better use of the available time, make meal arrangements in advance.

SECTION 5—SPONSORSHIP

Emmaus Ministries takes a different approach to recruitment than many church-related efforts. For its Walk to Emmaus and Chrysalis ministries, Emmaus uses a one-on-one method that is more consistent with the movement's message: sponsorship.

Emmaus Community members want to share the gift of their Emmaus Ministries experience with others; sponsorship provides them a caring, disciplined way to do so, enabling God's gift of grace to be passed on through the Emmaus movement. The fact that the Emmaus experience passes from person to person reflects the relational nature of God and the manner in which God purposefully reaches out to people through people. The personal character of sponsorship underlines God's personal care and commitment to each participant. Sponsors help make the Emmaus experience an act of sacrificial love from beginning to end—something more than the usual church retreat or religious education function.

Many Communities take sponsorship for granted. The members assume that everyone knows the *how* and *why* of sponsorship. Sometimes the Community discusses sponsorship only in regard to the number of participants signed up for an event. However, good sponsorship is the very reason healthy Communities rarely cancel Emmaus events for lack of participants. Good sponsorship is vital to the Emmaus movement in every Community; therefore, every Emmaus Community continually educates its members on the role and importance of good sponsorship.

The Walk to Emmaus and Chrysalis ministries use the sponsorship model described in this section, while the Face to Face and Journey to the Table ministries employ a recruitment model led by the host or sponsoring organization. Although Face to Face and Journey to the Table do not require sponsors, Emmaus Ministries Communities encourage their members, when appropriate, to extend invitations to persons to participate in these ministries and to support participants of these ministries' events in ways similar to those of a sponsor. In this way, the person-to-person, relational nature of sharing the Emmaus experience may extend to these ministries as well.

SPONSORSHIP TRAINING

Day Four: The Pilgrim's Continued Journey contains a chapter on sponsorship that would promote excellent discussion in every Community. Holding sponsorship workshops as part of monthly Gatherings prior to scheduled Emmaus events supports and encourages Community members to follow through with their intention to sponsor. Communities also discuss sponsorship at follow-up meetings with recent participants after Emmaus Ministries events. One resource titled *Sponsorship* gives a detailed explanation of the *whys*, *whens*, and *hows* of effective sponsorship.

An extended workshop on sponsorship could include a talk on sponsorship by a leader (see below), group discussion and group responses to the presentation, individual time in groups to reflect upon and share with one another the names of persons whom God is prompting each to sponsor, and Communion where persons offer to give the gift of Emmaus to those whom God has brought to mind. This type of meeting will broaden the base of those in the Emmaus Community who choose to sponsor intentionally from event to event.

The following talk outline reviews sponsorship. Leaders may present this outline as a whole or in parts as a series.

Sponsorship: The Most Important Job of All

Most Communities take sponsorship for granted; the members assume that everyone knows the how and why of sponsorship. Often Communities fail to discuss sponsorship except in reference to the number of participants signed up for an event. Yet sponsorship is the most important job in Emmaus, and all members take responsibility for this area of ministry. It involves more than simply signing up people. The Community leaders cannot overemphasize the significance of educating its Community about good sponsorship. The quality of sponsorship influences the participants, the health of the Emmaus movement, and the churches affected by the movement.

- Good sponsorship uses discernment in inviting or recruiting participants. Good sponsors do not set out simply to recruit anyone with a willingness to attend.

- Good sponsorship is the first act of agape before the Emmaus event ever begins; a participant's experience of his or her Emmaus Ministries event begins with how the Community handles sponsorship.

- Good sponsorship undergirds the Emmaus Ministries event with sacrificial love on behalf of each participant. Sponsors embody the personal commitment of the Community to each participant and provide personal acts of agape during the event for the participants. These acts of agape include prayer, agape letters, supportive presence at Candlelight and Closing, and follow-up.

- Good sponsorship offers a strong link to the participants' Fourth Day experience after each event. Sponsors stand ready to answer participants' questions, be faithful friends, and provide perspective. Sponsors guide participants to reunion groups, encourage them to revitalize their involvement in their churches and church groups, and help them sponsor others to attend an Emmaus Ministries event.

- Good sponsorship grounds a healthy, effective Emmaus movement that fulfills its true purpose: continued faith formation of the participants, the development of Christian leaders, and the renewal of the church in ministry.

Why do we sponsor? What is our aim?

A sponsor does not aim to "get all my friends to go," to fill up the event roster, to fix people's problems, or to reproduce his or her religious experience in others. Rather, the sponsor aims to bring spiritual revitalization to Christians who, in turn, will bring new life and vision to the work of the church in their congregations, homes, schools, workplaces, and Communities. Sponsorship supports the church's efforts to help Christians, young and old alike, grow spiritually—to build up the body of Christ. Sponsors need to evaluate their motive for sponsoring to ensure its consistency with this aim.

For the Chrysalis ministry, a number of additional hopes and prayers for young persons can motivate sponsorship. These include giving young persons the gift of time apart

- to experience the accepting and healing grace of God through Christian community,
- to realize that they are precious to God and are on this earth for a holy purpose,
- to discuss with nonjudgmental peers and mature Christian adults their questions and struggles as young persons,
- to hear anew the gospel of God's love in Jesus Christ and the basics of Christian faith and life,
- to make friends with other youth who share the faith and will support one another in living as Christians,
- to develop relationships with mature Christian adults, relationships that might extend beyond the three days,
- to strengthen their decision to follow Jesus,
- to better prepare themselves to live as Christian witnesses in home, school, church, and community,
- to learn what goes into building their lives and relationships on a solid foundation,
- to bring new vitality to the church youth group upon returning,
- to inspire the sponsorship of other youth,
- to energize the body of Christ through young people whose hearts are on fire with the love of Christ.

Ages of participants

The Emmaus Ministries include spiritual formation and renewal programs for several different life stages, which does not necessarily translate well to a specific age. A good sponsor considers the suitability of the ministry program for the life stage of the prospective participant.

- Chrysalis is for secondary (high school) young persons, fifteen to eighteen years old. These years are a critical time in a person's spiritual formation. Chrysalis is especially meaningful for young people who are ready to think about and discuss the realities and struggles of life on a more adult level: What am I going to do with my life? What kind of person do I want to become? What do I believe? What kind of relationships are lasting and most meaningful? What does it mean to live as a Christian, and how can I do it?

  Common experience demonstrates that young people who are not yet tenth graders (at least the summer prior to tenth grade) will benefit from waiting and be sponsored with their age group. Developmentally ready young people will gain immensely more from Chrysalis when in tune with the life experiences of the other youth participants. Sponsoring participants who are too young can sometimes detract from the value of the three days for the age group for which Chrysalis is intended.

- Journey to the Table is specifically designed for young adults, eighteen to thirty-five years, a time of life when many changes and transitions are occurring. It provides a place for young adults to raise questions and allow peers to share their experience, learning, and openness to how God and others may be working in their journey of faith. Journey to the Table encourages young adults to explore their faith, build relationships, and create spaces of Christian action in a transitory time of life.

- Walk to Emmaus is for adults eighteen years and older who are more established in a local church. Walk to Emmaus seeks to inspire, challenge, and equip adult leaders for Christian action in their homes, places of work, and communities.

- Face to Face is an experience in the tradition of The Walk to Emmaus designed specifically for seniors, sixty years and older. The Walk to Emmaus model is adjusted to accommodate ages and physical circumstances of the Face to Face audience. The life stage of senior constituents, their life settings, and their stamina dictate these adjustments. While most of The Walk to Emmaus talks are part of Face to Face, the ministry has added content meaningful to seniors.

Whom do we sponsor?

Community members' awareness of and commitment to the purpose of Emmaus influences whom they choose to sponsor and how they sponsor.

The Walk to Emmaus is for active Christians and church members whose personal renewal will bring fresh energy, commitment, and vision to the church and everyday environments for Christ's sake. Those sponsored could include the following:

- *church leaders (pastors and laypersons)* who will bring new vision, commitment, and understanding to their congregations and who need the renewal and grace that Emmaus channels;

- *dependable church members* who serve as the quiet backbone of the church;

- less active members who need their awareness of grace rekindled and their commitments renewed;
- *Christians who hunger for "something more"* and who want to grow spiritually;
- *members and leaders who represent a cross-section of the church* and will help Emmaus remain theologically sound, centered on the essentials of common faith and open to different perspectives;
- *other respected laypersons and clergypersons* whose participation, support, and leadership will encourage others to attend an Emmaus Ministries event and will build a sound, balanced leadership base for the movement in the community; and
- *members of diverse congregations, denominations, and ethnic groups.*

Young adults who previously attended a Chrysalis event and possibly have served on other Chrysalis events or activities, may express a desire to attend a Walk to Emmaus event. If they have not already served on a Walk to Emmaus Conference Room Team, they may be sponsored to attend a Walk to Emmaus event.

For Chrysalis, consider the following as likely candidates:

- *Young people who already attend church and youth groups.* Chrysalis is designed for young people who are actively involved in their churches. Youth pastors and adult leaders of youth, as well as key leaders in the youth program, can identify youth who are ready to grow by attending an event like Chrysalis. Sponsoring active church youth benefits the youth and the church. Chrysalis reinforces and vitalizes the faith-formation experiences that the church provides for young people. Chrysalis supplements the church's efforts to provide Christian formation opportunities.

  Moreover, church youth continue to support Chrysalis, do acts of agape (providing baked goods, carpooling, anything helpful that will aid a young person's Chrysalis experience), sponsor other young people, and attend Chrysalis events. Young people who are not connected with a church seldom follow through in supporting Chrysalis after the three days. Church-related young people are the backbone of the program.

- *Leaders in the church youth group.* Youth with leadership abilities will bring infectious energy and vision to their church groups. Their testimony will convince others of the value of participating. Intentional sponsorship of youth leaders will pay off for everyone.

- *Mature youth and campus leaders.* When campus leaders participate and find the experience meaningful, others want to do likewise. Chrysalis builds upon their natural leadership abilities and calls them to be a positive Christian influence.

- *Youth with fledgling faith or limited Christian background.* Chrysalis can focus the Christian message for such youth and give them an opportunity to respond to the gospel, perhaps for the first time. But Chrysalis is appropriate for them only when they genuinely desire to know more about Christ and the life of faith.

- *Church youth with no involvement in the youth group activities.* Chrysalis can help them connect with the other youth and may offer the solid experience they seek. But again, they should not be sponsored unless they desire to learn more about the Christian faith.

- *Youth of various races, economic backgrounds, and churches.* In Chrysalis, young people come to see that they are one in Christ and that their true identity transcends ethnic, cultural, denominational, and economic differences. Breaking out of a closed circle of friends and associations and sponsoring people from various backgrounds enhances the Chrysalis experience and spreads Chrysalis to new friendship networks.

- *Friends from school or elsewhere who are not part of the church but who show evidence of a desire to meet Christ and to grow spiritually.* Sponsors of these young people commit to helping them establish a relationship with their churches and youth groups before and especially after Chrysalis.

An Emmaus Ministries event is right for many people—but not for everyone. The religious background or emotional condition of some people may make Emmaus an unwise discipleship tool for them. Other persons may lack suitability for sponsorship to an Emmaus Ministries event because of the negative effect they might have on the event or the divisive influence they could bring to the church. Sponsorship requires sensitivity to these factors. Some examples of questionable sponsorship are these:

- Non-Christians or persons with no interest in the Christian faith or the church.
- Christians whose theology and/or practice notably differs from the traditional theology and practice represented by Emmaus. This includes Christians who have specific dietary restrictions and sabbath celebrations that the Emmaus experience cannot provide, members of groups who will feel a need to defend the uniqueness of their beliefs throughout the event, and persons who do not share belief in traditional doctrines of the faith basic to the major denominations of the church and to Emmaus Ministries.
- Persons undergoing an emotional crisis (for example, family breakup, job loss, severe grief) or who are psychologically unstable.
- Persons whose behavior pattern is to disrupt. Sponsors require assurance that the people they sponsor want to attend for the right reasons. Young people who attend Chrysalis need enough maturity to behave appropriately and to cooperate with the flow of the entire event. Otherwise, they will hinder the experience for everyone else. Chrysalis teams are not equipped to deal with major discipline problems nor is Chrysalis designed to "fix" chronic behavior problems.
- Persons whose family members do not want them to participate. Sponsors do not allow the Emmaus experience to become a point of division between a person and his or her spouse, or between a young person and his or her parent(s).
- Persons who decide not to attend an Emmaus Ministries event after being presented the opportunity. A potential sponsor need not feel like a failure if a prospect says no. Perhaps

the timing is not right. Perhaps God will renew the person in another way. Remember, the Emmaus experience is not every Christian's way to renewal.

- "Church-hoppers," members who frequently have an axe to grind with the church; persons who will use Emmaus as a tool to divide the body, to further their own theological agendas, or who will create an "Emmaus church."

- Persons who are always seeking another spiritual high or experience to help them "arrive."

Two kinds of sponsorship: wise and unwise

Wise sponsorship is purposeful and prayerful; unwise sponsorship is haphazard and undiscerning. Wise sponsorship eventually will produce a balanced, theologically centered movement of the Holy Spirit, which is integrated into the life of the church in the community, and which is honored by a variety of churches as an effective instrument for conveying God's grace, the call to committed discipleship, and our unity in Christ.

Unwise sponsorship eventually will produce a harvest that becomes more a burden than a blessing for the church: a movement that has become a religious fringe group or a parachurch apart from the established church in the community. At best, such groups benefit the individuals involved, having no impact upon or relationship with the churches in the community, thus forfeiting the purpose of the Emmaus movement. At worst, such groups benefit themselves at the expense of the church, breeding division instead of unity within the body of Christ and intolerance instead of tolerance among Christians of different religious expressions.

How do we sponsor?

The Emmaus *Sponsorship* book contains a chapter on "Responsibilities of the Sponsor." That chapter elaborates on these steps in sponsoring a prospective participant:

1. *PRAY! PRAY! Then pray some more!*

2. *Discern whom God wants you to sponsor.* Pray about those persons you would like to sponsor and others whom God would lead you to sponsor. For Chrysalis, work with another sponsor to prayerfully consider sponsoring more than one young person from a church so that they will have friends with whom to share the event and its follow-up.

3. *Continue to spend time in prayer.* Pray for the person's openness to God's call to discipleship rather than how to persuade him or her to attend an Emmaus event. Trust God to motivate the persons brought to mind.

4. *Make an appointment.* Discuss with potential candidates the purpose and benefits of Emmaus, what you experienced as benefits, some positive aspects of the event, and the follow-up dimension. For The Walk to Emmaus, if the candidate is married, include both spouses when making the appointment and in the follow-up discussion. For Chrysalis, also make an appointment with the candidate's parents or guardians to share in depth the basic elements and value of Chrysalis and to alleviate any concerns they may have.

5. *Extend an invitation and seek a commitment.* Invite the candidate to attend for the sake of a more vital relationship with Jesus Christ. Convey the offer of a wonderful gift rather than stressing that he or she needs to go. Explain the cost and ask the prospective candidate to commit by filling out the application form. If the person is married, speak with both partners and encourage an equal commitment by both.

6. *Make preparations for your candidate.* Continue to pray for your prospective participant, and enlist the support of his or her pastor. Take steps to collect personal agape letters— eight to twelve for Walk to Emmaus and ten to twenty for Chrysalis. Do not ask the team to deliver personal gifts to your participant, from you or anyone else, during the event.

7. *Make sacrifices for your candidate.* Plan to handle whatever responsibilities will need attention on behalf of your candidate during the event such as house-sitting, babysitting, watering plants, picking up mail, feeding pets, or just checking in with a spouse to see if any help is needed. Consider tasks you can undertake that will make it possible for the candidate to attend.

8. *Support the event during the three days.* Sign up for the 72-Hour Prayer Vigil, and be present at Sponsors' Hour, Candlelight, and Closing. For Chrysalis, invite the participant's parents to Parents' Meeting, Send-Off, Sponsors' Hour, and/or Closing, when appropriate.

9. *Encourage the participant in his or her Fourth Day involvement.* Give your friend an opportunity to talk about the three-day experience and what it meant to him or her. Help the participant find a reunion or Next Steps group, or be prepared to start a group with him or her for a period of time until others join the group. Take the participant to Community Gatherings as your guest for a couple of months. Help him or her feel included.

10. *Help your participant act on new commitments.* Help the participant reenter his or her church and follow through on fresh hopes and dreams, decisions, and changes he or she feels called by God to make. For a young person not active in a church, invite him or her to become part of your church and youth group.

11. *Inform the participant of ways to serve the Emmaus Community.* Encourage his or her support of upcoming Emmaus Ministries events through prayer and by serving behind-the-scenes. Explain and model progressive servanthood so that he or she may work toward serving on a future leadership team.

12. *Help your participant sponsor others.* Offer assistance the first time he or she sponsors someone else. Explain the responsibilities and expectations of sponsors. Above all, be a model sponsor yourself.

Sponsorship is an act of love for God, for the participants, for the Emmaus Community, and for the church. It is a living demonstration of agape love. Through sponsorship, we become instruments of God's design and prevenient grace.

Who can sponsor?

Any person who has participated in an Emmaus ministry or other recognized three-day movement event can sponsor a person to any Emmaus ministry event so long as he or she (1) understands the aim and responsibilities of sponsorship and (2) can fulfill them for the person he or she would sponsor.

- For Chrysalis, it is important that the sponsor be someone the potential participant knows and looks up to; when this is the case, a young person will more likely attend Chrysalis and stay involved.

- Church leaders such as pastors and ministry directors make excellent sponsors because they know the persons who are ready to make the most of their Emmaus Ministries event and will strengthen the church by their participation.

- In many cases, the best sponsors are people who have attended an Emmaus Ministries event and want to sponsor their own family members (siblings, parents, children, etc.). In other cases, particularly for a young person planning to attend Chrysalis, parents may feel better about encouraging other adults to sponsor their child.

- In some cases, young or inexperienced sponsors need to be linked up with experienced sponsors in order to ensure follow-through on all the responsibilities of good sponsorship. Persons who only recently attended an Emmaus Ministries event would better serve with the assistance of an experienced cosponsor. Registrars need some sensitivity to sponsors who require assistance.

Given the importance of sponsorship, Boards of Directors may develop local guidelines and reasonable expectations to ensure responsible sponsorship. For example, Emmaus Ministries application forms may have a provision that potential sponsors are to give evidence that they understand and accept the responsibilities of sponsorship for their candidate. Registrars may expect and ask potential sponsors to indicate that they have attended a sponsorship training session, if such opportunities are accessible throughout the year at Gatherings, Community education days, or in other ways.

Potential sponsors who have participated in another valid expression of Emmaus may need to confirm a degree of contact with or involvement in the local Emmaus Community and evidence an understanding of Emmaus and sponsorship.

Sponsors do not serve as team members on Emmaus Ministries events with people they are sponsoring. If a person has already committed to sponsor, he or she declines the invitation to be a team member. If sponsors choose to serve as team members, they find others who will sponsor their candidates. Team members *cannot* support a participant during the event in the manner intended, such as Sponsors' Hour, the Prayer Vigil, and Candlelight.

Confusing the roles of team member and sponsor in relationship with a participant diminishes the value of both roles:

- On the one hand, team members who also sponsor often cannot serve without anticipating, hovering, or being distracted by a special interest in the responses of "their" participants.
- On the other hand, the hopes and expectations of their ever-present sponsors on the team may limit participants' freedom to respond, a likelihood that is antithetical to the principles of Emmaus.

Sponsors do not serve as team members on the same event, and participants should not see their sponsors serving "behind-the-scenes" as support persons during the event. The absence of the sponsors gives the participants the space they need for their own interaction with and experience of God during the event.

CHRYSALIS PARENTS' MEETING

For parents who lack familiarity with Emmaus or another three-day movement, Chrysalis is new and different. Even for those who have participated in a Walk to Emmaus event, Chrysalis is unique both in its design and in young people's responses to the experience.

Some parents need reassurance that Chrysalis is not a cult or a secret society. Some may have the unrealistic expectation that Chrysalis will immediately or thoroughly change their young person. Still others may require affirmation of their critical, God-given role in their youth's faith journey thus far.

Though the sponsors' responsibilities include explaining Chrysalis to the parents, many Communities find that a general Parents' Meeting helps foster genuine support and alleviates parental anxiety.

The Parents' Meeting reinforces parents' understanding of Chrysalis, gives them more information about the program, allows them an opportunity to ask questions, prepares them for their young person's responses, and suggests ways they can support their youth after the event.

The Parents' Meeting is held before the Chrysalis event or at the same time as Sponsors' Hour. The Community Lay Director and/or Spiritual Director or someone they appoint leads the meeting.

When a young person's application to Chrysalis is accepted, his or her parents receive an invitation by mail to the Parents' Meeting. Later, sponsors contact parents about the meeting and, if necessary, provide transportation.

A Parents' Meeting typically lasts about an hour.

Suggested Parents' Meeting Agenda

1. Welcome and introduction(s)
   - Parents
   - Chair of the Board of Directors
   - Community Spiritual Director and/or Lay Director

(Explain the relationship of the Community Lay Director and Spiritual Director to the Chrysalis event)

2. Purpose and Nature of Chrysalis
   - *Overview of the Event*
     - Fifteen talks—five youth, five adults, five clergy
     - Relationship talks
     - Recreation
     - Food
     - Association with other youth in the faith
     - Interaction with other adults in the faith
     - All needs met during the event
   - *The Fourth Day*
     - Follow-up with Next Steps groups, share groups, Bible study groups
     - Gatherings
     - Positive relationship to local church involvement

3. Chrysalis Event Closing Service
   - Invite parents or guardians; inform them of day, time, location
   - Explain what to expect from the Closing service and the youth
   - Tell what will be going on during the service:
     - Singing
     - Sharing by the youth
     - Holy Communion

4. What's Next?
   - Explain that Chrysalis does not try to make saints of young people but simply builds on the foundation the parents and the church have established to pass on the Christian faith. The young people may come back changed, but change is difficult. Suggest ways parents can support their youth after the event:
     - Do not hold the Chrysalis experience over their heads if they slip back into old habits.
     - Give affirmation and support.
     - Help youth maintain their associations with new friends in the faith.
     - Help them translate their new commitment into strengthened involvement in the church, if possible.
     - Be patient with initial exuberance and enthusiasm; respond with support and tolerance.
     - Talk with them about their experiences if they are willing.

- Share your own faith experiences with them.
- Introduce The Walk to Emmaus as a possibility for parents and guardians who have not attended a three-day experience. Have available Walk to Emmaus information sheets and the next Walk to Emmaus event dates.

SPONSORS' HOUR

After the Send-Off, once the participants have left the assembly room to begin their event, the sponsors and others present gather in the chapel for a time of prayer for the participants and their experience. For Chrysalis, if the Parents' Meeting is to follow the Sponsors' Hour, the parents of the participants will take part in the Sponsors' Hour as well. The Community Spiritual Director or a board member leads Sponsors' Hour or arranges for someone in the community to lead it.

This brief service consists of prayer for each of the participants by name. The leader may read aloud the name of each participant. As a name is read, his or her sponsor walks to the front where the participants' crosses are draped across the altar. The sponsor takes a cross for his or her participant and hangs it across the arm of a large standing cross. The individual crosses will remain there throughout the event as a symbolic focus of prayer in the Prayer Chapel. Those gathered pray silently for each participant as his or her cross is carried forward. If a sponsor is not present and did not arrange for a proxy, any Community member may spontaneously stand in for the sponsor and carry the cross forward.

A MODEL SPONSOR

The following is a statement from Jean Johnson Green, a member of the Nashville Upper Room Emmaus Community. She went through Cursillo in 1979 and has been the registrar for the Emmaus Community, has served on the Board of Directors, is a past Weekend Lay Director, and has served in The Upper Room Emmaus Ministries Office as Assistant Lay Director. Her practice serves as a good model for us all.

Sponsorship is like being a godparent. A godparent doesn't just stand with a person at the front of the church but helps him or her grow in the spiritual life. One time a woman couldn't [attend an Emmaus event] because she had a one-month-old baby. She said, "There's no way I can go because I have no one to keep the children." And I said, "Oh, yes, you do!"

During the three days, I always try—if family's involved—to let the family members know that I've seen the participant who is doing well and having a good time. Sharing information about the spouse is especially important to the wives when the husbands are going through, because the wives haven't been through yet and don't know what it's all about. I took one woman out to dinner that Friday night.

After their events, I strongly feel that you call the persons you sponsor. Sometimes people are excited to change the world, but the fire can die down if it's not fed. As a sponsor my job is to see that the fire is fed and grows. It doesn't take that much—a phone call, an invitation to a Gathering. Maybe instead of my going to Candlelight, I keep the kids so the couple can go or so they can work in the kitchen on a subsequent Emmaus event.

I also try to get my participant together with some other recent participants to start a group reunion. I meet with them several times and show them what it's all about. I have my own group, but I help the new group get started. When I don't see the persons I've sponsored at a Gathering, my responsibility isn't to pester them but to maintain contact, offering to go with them the next time and maybe having dinner with them afterward.

SECTION 6—
FOURTH DAY

As explained in Section I, *The Emmaus Story*, the Emmaus movement is part of a larger three-day movement made up of organizations that conduct spiritual renewal events. Most—but not all—of the events held by these organizations cover three days, so *Fourth Day* has become a term used by the three-day movement to describe the participant's life after the renewal event.

The Walk to Emmaus does occur over three days' time and refers to the life of the participant after the event as Fourth Day, but Chrysalis refers to this time as Next Steps. The Journey to the Table ministry event, structured as seven sections (twenty-four hours of instructional time) that may or may not be offered consecutively, does not use a specific term for the participant's life after the event. However, it does encourage event participants to further their spiritual growth and development by continuing the cycle of hearing from and responding to the Lord and then debriefing with others. The Face to Face ministry event, structured as eight half-day sections that may occur over the period of a week or more, uses the term *Next Day* to refer to the participant's life after the event. Since all Emmaus ministries are part of the three-day movement, the term *Fourth Day* will apply to the participant's life after attending any of these Emmaus Ministries' events.

Community members understand that the goal of an Emmaus event is not just a great mountaintop experience but a revitalized and sustained spiritual relationship with Christ and the church as the participants live out their Fourth Day as disciples of Jesus Christ in the world. A strong follow-up emphasis by the Emmaus Community sustains participants' renewed discipleship after their event.

In healthy Emmaus Communities, this Fourth Day perspective and emphasis involves helping Community members stay connected with their local church organizations as a common faith community and in small support groups for mutual encouragement, guidance, and accountability. For The Walk to Emmaus and Face to Face ministries, these small support groups are called group reunions; for the Chrysalis ministry, they are called Next Steps groups; and for the Journey to the Table ministry, they are called Table Groups. The term *accountability group* will refer to any of these Emmaus ministry support groups.

This section describes elements of the Emmaus Fourth Day follow-up emphasis and how an Emmaus Community may develop and encourage them. These elements include the Fourth

Day Follow-up Meeting, Accountability Groups, Meetings of the Community, and the Emmaus and Church Partnership.

FOURTH DAY MEMBERS

When a person completes an Emmaus event, he or she is considered to be a Fourth Day member of the Emmaus movement. Occasionally, an unexpected circumstance (sickness, medical emergency, or family emergency) causes a participant to withdraw from an Emmaus event before its completion. The timing of the participant's departure impacts his or her status with Emmaus as follows:

- If the participant leaves the event *prior to* the Candlelight service, he or she *is not* considered a Fourth Day member of the Emmaus movement and receives encouragement to attend a future event in its entirety.

- If the participant leaves the event *after* the Candlelight service, he or she *is* considered to be a Fourth Day member of the Emmaus movement.

Upon becoming a Fourth Day member of the Emmaus movement, a participant is also considered to be a member of the local Emmaus Community that sponsored the event.

Participants in an Emmaus Ministries event *not* sponsored by an Emmaus Community (such as a Journey to the Table event sponsored by a campus ministry) become Fourth Day members of the Emmaus movement and are welcome to become members of one or more local Emmaus Communities simply by expressing their desire to do so. This connection with local Emmaus Communities provides a flow of information and opportunities to participate in Emmaus Fourth Day follow-up activities.

FOURTH DAY FOLLOW-UP MEETING

Shortly after each Emmaus-sponsored event, the Community hosts a Fourth Day Follow-up Meeting with recent event participants to encourage them to form accountability groups, to aid them in their Fourth Day experience since their event, and to orient them to the Emmaus Community and its leaders. This Fourth Day Follow-up Meeting is critical for Community-sponsored events of all Emmaus ministries.

Communities may construct their Follow-up Meetings in various ways, often including get-acquainted activities, music, drama, a potluck dinner, Holy Communion, or other ways to create a welcoming atmosphere and open communication. However, the aim of Follow-up Meetings is to convey basic information through one of several ways:

Reviewing. A leader spends a few minutes outlining memorable moments of the recent Emmaus event(s) to remind everyone of the basic message of the Emmaus movement and to help the new Community members recall their experiences.

Sharing. A leader invites new Community members to tell about the return to their everyday world and how their Fourth Day is going so far, be it joyful and challenging or difficult and discouraging. Participants stand to speak voluntarily, in any order, and are encouraged to take no more than two or three minutes each. This gives them a chance to renew relationships, to laugh together, and to show support for those who have encountered difficulties.

Grouping. A leader reminds new Community members of the benefit of accountability groups for keeping the spirit of their experience alive and for maintaining relationships that encourage them to live as disciples of Jesus Christ. After a brief presentation about the value of the accountability group from a personal standpoint (for Chrysalis, it helps to have a young person speak), new Community members not yet in a group are given the opportunity to form or join one. Those interested may gather in one part of the meeting space to discuss possible places and times to meet. They may be asked to indicate via a sign-up sheet what time blocks during a week serves them best to meet, or they may be asked to find other potential group members by gathering around a large piece of paper (of several taped on the walls around the room) that displays the portion of the day and day of the week when they could possibly meet. Many options exist.

As time permits, the newly formed groups or random groupings of three persons participate in a time of small-group sharing by responding to one or more questions from the accountability group card. Leaders ensure that experienced Community members assist the newly formed groups. This activity gives the new members additional experience with the accountability group meeting. For a Follow-up Meeting after a Chrysalis event, the presence of local church Chrysalis representatives increases the effectiveness of the meeting and other follow-up efforts.

Informing. New Community members should receive, or be encouraged to purchase, a Team Manual, which includes information about the Emmaus movement, the leaders, and Emmaus ministries. A speaker introduces them to Community Gatherings and invites all new members to the next one in a welcoming message. New members receive instruction on the purpose of Emmaus, the importance of good sponsorship, the opportunity to support upcoming Emmaus events, and the commitment involved in being on a team. Every member of the Emmaus Community needs information to participate responsibly.

The Follow-up Chair or other local Emmaus ministry leader takes responsibility for the Follow-up Meeting, which includes encouraging all participants from the most recent event(s) and their sponsors to attend. If the meeting follows a Men's Walk to Emmaus event and a Women's Walk to Emmaus event will be held soon, the spouses of the recent participants may attend a separate meeting held at the same time. All team members are expected to be present, and other Community members and leaders are welcome.

The Follow-Up Chair may approach the Follow-Up Meeting in several ways, each of which has advantages.

Tuesday Evening Following the Event

One approach holds the Fourth Day Follow-up Meeting on the Tuesday evening after an event, a common practice for Walk to Emmaus and other events that conclude on a weekend.

Below is a sample agenda:

7:15 p.m.   Welcome, explanation of the agenda, brief review of the recently held Emmaus events. (If applicable, the Lay Director of the upcoming Women's Walk to Emmaus event meets separately with the spouses in another room)

7:20 p.m.   Singing and opening prayer.

7:25 p.m.   Introductions by name and table.

7:35 p.m.   Fourth Day sharing; after each person speaks, the group supports that person with applause.

8:05 p.m.   A song for transition.

8:10 p.m.   Accountability group encouragement: the Follow-up Chair or a designate shares briefly about the value of the accountability group.

The Follow-Up Chair identifies the Community members present who are willing to help form new groups. Provide a way for persons to indicate their desire to form or join a group (such as sign-up sheets). The Follow-Up Chair responds to the expressed interest by organizing new groups, providing help from experienced Community members, or including new members in established groups.

If time permits, have all participate in small-group sharing using one or two questions from the accountability group card.

8:25 P.M.   Introduction of other Emmaus Community leaders and explanation of their roles, explanation of ways to stay informed and involved with the Emmaus Community, announcements about upcoming Emmaus Community activities.

8:30 P.M.   Prayer requests, closing prayer and song.

The Fourth Day Follow-up Meeting lasts no longer than described here. If the meeting is subsequent to a Men's Walk to Emmaus event and includes a separate meeting for the spouses who will attend the upcoming Women's Walk to Emmaus event, care must be taken so that the meetings conclude at the same time.

Walk to Emmaus Pre-Event Meeting for Spouses

For the Fourth Day Follow-up Meeting following a Men's Walk to Emmaus event, the Follow-Up Chair and sponsors encourage the men to bring their spouses who will be pilgrims on the upcoming Women's Walk. Before the introductions, the Lay Director for the upcoming women's event leads the women to another room to provide basic information and to answer questions about the upcoming event. Above all, the Lay Director wants to allay any anxieties that may have arisen since their husbands' return from their event. The Lay Director plans an informal, one-hour meeting that includes introductions, a brief explanation of The Walk to Emmaus event and what to bring, a question-and-answer session, and time to visit.

The close of the women's meeting coincides with the closing of the men's Fourth Day Follow-Up Meeting. The women do not rejoin the men until both groups have finished their entire agenda, including the closing prayer and song. Be aware that the post-event enthusiasm of the men in song and prayer can generate new anxieties in the women.

An Evening Following a Set of Events

This approach involves the men and women participants in the Community's most recent events and eliminates the need for the pre-event meeting with spouses during the men's Follow-Up Meeting.

A Saturday Following a Set of Events

This approach involves the new members and the Community in a day of retreat and fellowship. It accomplishes all the aims of the evening Follow-Up Meeting but introduces the new and existing Community members to one another more fully. In addition to the above agenda, the day includes planned Fourth Day witnesses from several Community members and group discussions. It allows time for informal fellowship during lunch.

Local Clusters within Large Emmaus Communities

In some Emmaus Communities that cover a large geographical area, it may be unrealistic to gather the participants from the recent Emmaus Ministries events together for this purpose. Instead, new members come together in local clusters within the Emmaus Community, where they receive further orientation to Emmaus activities and are encouraged to join accountability groups.

ACCOUNTABILITY GROUPS / GROUP REUNIONS

Day Four: The Pilgrim's Continued Journey describes Emmaus accountability groups as "one of the chief values of the Emmaus movement—one of the greatest treasures [it] contains." A speaker during an Emmaus event introduces accountability groups as the means by which participants can persevere in grace during the Fourth Day.

An accountability group consists of two to six persons who meet regularly (weekly, biweekly) at a regular time for about an hour to support one another in living toward the Christian ideal of a grace-filled life. These groups may include persons who have attended an Emmaus event and those who have not. It is possible that a group may include persons who have attended different types of Emmaus events (Chrysalis, Journey to the Table, Face to Face). The group card that each participant receives at the close of the Emmaus event indicates the order of the meeting. The book *Day Four: The Pilgrim's Continued Journey* provides an excellent explanation and discussion of the accountability group concept, the group card format, criteria for forming groups, and the characteristics of an effective group.

Some Emmaus Communities have more success than others in forming accountability groups. Generally speaking, Communities report that one out of every three or four members participates in an accountability group.

The Key to Successful Accountability Groups

* *A Fourth Day perspective on Emmaus prevails* in Communities with successful accountability groups. These Communities measure the vitality of the Emmaus movement not

---

by the number of events or the number of participants but by the number of ongoing accountability groups among its members. Commitment to a Fourth Day understanding of the Emmaus goal is evident in the Community's leadership, teams, and sponsors.

- *Fourth Day is a priority among the Emmaus Community leadership.* Though everyone agrees in theory on the importance of accountability groups, the Emmaus Community leaders practice this method of living in grace. While every Board of Directors hopes that its event participants will form or join accountability groups, effective Boards discuss and act on this hope in concrete and creative ways. After an Emmaus Ministries event, the Board discusses its continuing responsibility to those who have just completed the event and monitors the effort to involve them in groups.

- *Sponsors commit to their participants' Fourth Day.* In successful Fourth Day Communities, sponsors understand their responsibilities. They know to recruit those who have a church base for building their life of discipleship, support them with agape, and are present for them at Candlelight and Closing. They also know the expectation of helping those they sponsor to find or form accountability groups, take them if necessary to the first few Community Gatherings after their Emmaus events, and assist them in acting out their renewed commitment to be intentional members of the body of Christ in their local church and Community. A Community trains sponsors in their Fourth Day responsibilities through written handouts, scheduled Community trainings, and presentations at Community Gatherings. Sponsors require ongoing education and encouragement in their role.

  For Chrysalis, whenever possible, encourage sponsorship of more than one person from the same church. This ensures that young people have companions after the event and increases the chances of starting accountability groups within congregations.

- *The value of accountability groups is made clear during the Emmaus Ministries events.* Speakers write their Emmaus event talks with a Fourth Day emphasis in mind. Because team members are usually in accountability groups, speakers for a number of the event talks may include passing references to the value of small-group support, especially in the talks given later in the event.

- In particular, the talk given by the event's lay team leader will address the spiritual and practical value of accountability groups, with the backing of the speaker's personal experience. Participants need to understand that these groups are for ordinary people, that they build on the friendships established during the event, and that they provide a base of support for the Fourth Day. During the talk, team members may demonstrate the accountability group concept with a three-minute role-play, so the participants can see the order and simplicity of the meeting. This enactment involves three team members and requires rehearsal. For the table discussion following the talk, a leader may instruct the tables to experience an accountability group session by following the group card format and sharing in response to some of the questions. The participants will have much to share at this point; their first experience with the accountability group format, though brief, will be positive.

Table leaders will speak from experience about accountability groups and bear witness to their value. This personal testimony can impress on the participants the value of an accountability group. Team-formation meetings include small-group time to give even team members who may not presently be in a group some recent experience with the concept as well as to develop relationships among the team.

- *Follow-Up or Fourth Day Committees are active.* Successful Fourth Day Communities have a committee chair on the Board of Directors or Ministry Leadership Committee who takes responsibility to help new Community members and others who are not in accountability groups to find or form groups. The Board and the Follow-Up chair act on the principle that every new Community member deserves a personal contact more than once to encourage involvement in an accountability group.

  When an Emmaus Community has several small towns in its geographical area, each town requires representation on the Follow-up Committee. These people assist in efforts to establish accountability groups in their locales.

Additional Ways to Encourage Accountability Groups

- Ask Table Leaders, in addition to sponsors, to follow up on the participants at their tables. Table Leaders get to know the participants well. They can honor those new friendships by making contact with the participants and helping them find or form new groups, perhaps with the others at their table.

  For the Chrysalis ministry, the youth-adult relationships the Chrysalis event fosters are significant. Young people need strong Christian role models and healthy relationships with adults who can be their spiritual friends. Adult team members commit to support and maintain contact with the Chrysalis participants for six months after their team involvement; if willing, they can initiate and guide the formation of accountability groups. Adult team members can take the initiative by calling some young people together for a first group meeting and exploring the possibility of regular meetings. They can also help simply by offering their homes for meetings and refreshments or by being a stable, guiding presence. Along with sponsors, the adult Table Leaders and other team members can encourage the Chrysalis participants to join accountability groups, stay connected to the community, and participate in their churches.

- Host a Fourth Day Follow-up Meeting in the days immediately after each event or set of events for all participants and sponsors. Most Communities employ this approach.

- Emphasize accountability groups at Community Gatherings. At Community Gatherings foster opportunities for uninvolved people to get together and form new groups. Consider having veteran accountability group members share their experience of the value of their groups and their wisdom on how to keep a group vital over the long haul.

- Offer workshops on accountability groups during Community training sessions. A good resource for a workshop is titled *The Group Reunion.*

- Consider special times when several accountability groups can meet simultaneously in different rooms at the same location. This approach can offer a great sense of support and camaraderie. Early Saturday morning is a common meeting time for groups that may meet in a church hall or at the same location. Wednesday after work or school is also a popular meeting time for several groups, followed by a brief service of Holy Communion for all.

- Do not limit participation in accountability groups to those who have been on an Emmaus Ministries event. Accountability groups are spiritual support groups for *any* Christian on the journey of faith who desires to live a life of accountable discipleship. The purpose of the group is not to talk about Emmaus but to share faith and life in Christ.

  Times and places of accountability group meetings in churches can be published in the church meeting schedule alongside other activities and meetings; this may encourage church or youth group members who have yet to attend an Emmaus event to contact members of the accountability group to find out more. Sometimes a person's participation in an accountability group precedes participation in an Emmaus event. If possible, suggest that accountability groups be part of ongoing church group activities or studies. At the beginning of or toward the end of a more broadly focused program, invite people into small groups to share more personally using the Emmaus accountability group format.

  The accountability group represents a recovery and restoration of a small-group dynamic for deepening discipleship in the church. It serves as one of Emmaus's greatest gifts to the church. The Emmaus Community exemplifies extravagant generosity with the gifts God has given through the Emmaus movement.

- Those seeking involvement in an accountability group could place an ad in a Community email or other notification that would include suitable meeting days and times as well as a contact.

- Communities may place a premium on accountability group participation or its equivalent when selecting team members from the Emmaus Community.

- Active young people may have difficulty finding regular times to meet. Knowing that getting youth together may be hard (due to school and work schedules, not being able to drive, and so forth), Chrysalis leaders can develop some creative options for participating in a Chrysalis Next Steps accountability group:
  - Neighborhood Open House

    An adult opens his or her home weekly to a Next Steps group on the same night and same time; the adult may or may not be part of the group, depending on the consensus of the group. An adult may facilitate the first one or two meetings in order to serve as a role model, but after that, a youth may lead the meeting. The meetings are one hour in length, and food is not necessary. Understand and accept that the same youth will not always attend.

  - Before- or After-School Meeting

Ask high school officials if the school will provide space for a weekly group meeting; if the school requires a teacher or parent to sponsor such a group, find a teacher or parent from that school who is part of the local Emmaus Community. Be respectful of the school and its staff: Start and end the meeting on time, and leave the room in the same or better condition than it was before the meeting.

- Youth Group

  A church youth group could be a Next Steps group. Ask the youth director or minister about allowing the Next Steps group meeting at a different time than the church youth group. Or see if the youth director/minister would consider devoting thirty minutes of youth group time to small-group sharing.

- Help form accountability groups among persons who have church or school in common. Accountability group members having their church in common strengthens the church the members' bonds with their church and facilitates the ability to meet regularly. For young people, it can strengthen their church's youth group, the church's role in sponsoring youth to attend an Emmaus event, and the church's perceived value of the Emmaus ministries for their youth. An accountability group made up of young people from the same school can more easily meet together before or after school. School is often a stronger point of identification and contact than church, especially in cities with several schools. This helps young people connect their faith with their daily lives and provides a witness for Christ in the school environment.

Reminders for an Effective Accountability Group

- *Plan a specific time and place.* Plan a specific day, time, frequency, meeting length, and place for regular meetings. While these specifics may need to vary from time to time, make sure all group members know the agreed-upon schedule.

- *Commit yourselves.* Commit not only to God but to one another. Be regular in your attendance and participation. When you feel like it least, you may need it the most! You go not only to help yourself but also to help one another. When the group feels least valuable to you, it may be making a difference for someone else. With no commitment to be there for one another, the group will not develop in a healthy manner.

- *Prepare yourselves ahead of time.* Review the questions and your commitments before you arrive. Bring something to share. Expect Christ to be there awaiting your arrival, prepared to hear you and encourage you with a word you need to hear.

- *Practice your disciplines.* Take seriously the promises on your group card—piety, study, and action. Remember that the greatest source of dullness in groups is members who do not practice the disciplines during the week. If members have nothing to share or no practice to improve, they have no reason to meet. Challenge each person to take responsibility for his or her Christian growth. A group occasionally takes stock and asks, "Are we serious about the reasons for our group's meeting? Do we want to live in grace through the practice of piety, study, and action?"

- *Uphold one another.* Discourage superficial responses and be accountable to the members of the group for your Christian practice and growth. Remember one another's goals and plans for action. Ask about the past week's plans; celebrate successes, and forgive failures. Encourage the members of your accountability group. Be Christ for one another.

- *Pray for one another.* Intercede for the group members regularly, and be there for one another in times of need.

- *Focus on the service card.* Go section by section, allowing everyone to contribute his or her part. Then move on to the next section. Work through the whole card. If time is short, focus on particular questions for deeper sharing, accountability, and avoidance of superficiality. Honor the order, but don't be afraid to adjust it to meet the group's needs.

- *Retreat with one another.* Get together as a group once or twice a year for a quiet day of spiritual conversation, reflection on scripture, and prayer. Make this a time to share life goals and commitments. This time apart will deepen the value of the mutual support and accountability in the weekly meetings.

- *Plan your discipleship.* The group is a covenant relationship with friends committed to a life of piety, study, and action. Set personal goals with regard to your Christian devotion and discipleship. Share and test your goals with one another. Don't skip discussing your plans for the week to come. Pray for one another's perseverance.

- *Act as a group.* Make a specific plan to be in mission as a group, either in your church, through Emmaus agape acts, or in your community. This service will also deepen the bond and sense of companionship as Christians. Encourage the accountability groups for young people to come up with names for themselves to strengthen their identities as groups. This is a fun approach when groups first form, and it is similar to participants' naming their tables on the first day of the Chrysalis event.

- *Be spiritual friends.* A spiritual friend is one who will listen to you more deeply than you can listen to yourself; one who will help you be faithful to what is best within yourself. A spiritual friend is a friend with the Spirit and a friend with you. A spiritual friend helps you keep the fire burning within to be your best and remain faithful to God's call. Spiritual friends are the body of Christ for one another. They pray for one another daily and avoid self-righteous expectations and judgments. They are genuine with one another and maintain confidentiality at all times.

Causes of Weakness in Accountability Groups

- *Aimlessness.* The group card provides a format for meeting, an order for spiritual discipline, and an agenda for sharing. Eventually, members may need to clarify for themselves and one another their expectations of the group and their personal commitments to it. Otherwise, the sharing and sense of support level off; the group stops meeting its members' deeper needs. The group can die from superficiality because of neglect and unwillingness to talk about dissatisfaction with the group experience.

When a group first forms, it helps if the members personally answer the following questions aloud:

- What do I want from this accountability group experience and weekly discipline? What do I hope to gain?
- What is my commitment to God for which I need the group's support? Do I want to live in grace through the practice of piety, study, and action?
- What will be our commitment to one another?

Agree as a group to assess every six months (or as the need arises) the group's seriousness about its reasons for meeting, each person's commitment to live with spiritual discipline, and ways the group can become more effective for each member.

Group members will take their spiritual plan for the next week seriously, taking turns writing down each member's plans, asking about progress at the next meeting, and praying for one another to follow through on the plans.

- *Alterations.* Every accountability group experiences loss of members who move away, marry, get sick, die, change groups, or simply drop out. A group in this situation can exercise its faith by turning its liabilities into spiritual assets, realizing Christ has called its members to support one another in these circumstances.

  Those who move away are sent off with God's blessing; group members maintain contact with them through prayer and correspondence. When members are sick, the group meets at their bedside. When members change groups, their need is recognized without feelings of rejection and with prayer that God will meet their need. When members drop out, they are held in prayer during group meetings; group members keep in touch with them as friends, continuing to uphold them in their faith.

  Changes in the membership of an accountability group offer opportunities to welcome new individuals or to help start new groups if yours becomes too large.

- *Anemia.* Sometimes accountability groups or individuals within the group experience diminishing idealism, self-surrender, and charity for no apparent reason. This spiritual anemia may manifest itself as spiritual dullness or dryness in individuals or in the group, even when group members earnestly pursue their spiritual disciplines and their commitment to the group meeting. Often, however, when one member feels the group meeting is least worthwhile, another member feels it is most worthwhile. This dynamic underscores the importance of each one's commitment to regular participation. We come to the meetings not only for ourselves but to be there for the others and to make the group meeting possible for one another.

  Spiritual anemia can signal a lack of commitment to one another in the group. As Juan Hervas points out in the *Leader's Manual for Cursillos in Christianity*, the first weak link in a group is not the failure of the coldest member but too little response on the part of the most enthusiastic member. Group members exercise Christian love on behalf of others. But when we do not seek out missing members, do not show real concern or give a listening ear, do not look for remedies to group dullness, do not pray for one another or help one another live up to our hopes for ourselves, then the love that binds individual members into a Christian community is lacking.

Spiritual dullness can also signal God's desire that a person or group realize their "stuckness" in routine spiritual practices or narrow perspectives. Members may ask themselves and God through prayer and journaling whether God is calling for something new in their prayers, studies, and action, or in their relationships and commitments. Members seek awareness of a need, a question, or a challenge from God—individually or as a group—to lead them to new depths.

Spiritual dullness may signal spiritual gluttony, the eventual result of filling up on spiritual-growth experiences and knowledge for ourselves without also expending ourselves in love for others. We have no more room to receive from God until we empty ourselves in obedient love for the welfare of others.

Spiritual dryness may be God's way of withdrawing our familiar experiences of God's presence upon which we depend so we can learn to live more by faith than by feeling. We help one another trust God's presence and ask how God wants to strengthen our faith and love through this phase on our journey. Whatever the cause or interpretation of spiritual anemia, we persevere in the grace of Jesus Christ with the help of one another until grace prevails once again in our lives.

Common Questions about Accountability Groups

- *Should event team members and Emmaus Ministries leaders be required to participate in an accountability group?*

An accountability group is an integral part of the Emmaus model for living in grace. For team members and Community leaders to represent the Emmaus movement with integrity, they commit to the goals and practices of the method. Team Selection Committees may place a premium on participation in an accountability group when selecting team members. After all, teams teach most profoundly through the witness of their lives and practices. Various talks throughout an Emmaus Ministries event discuss authenticity in witness, the characteristics and value of an accountability group, and commitment to servanthood. Those presenting the talks commit to the concept and *practice* of the accountability group in their Fourth Day.

However, a Community can encourage the commitment of team members and Community leaders without being legalistic. A legalistic approach can squelch openness about participation, foster disregard for individual differences, and promote a narrow self-righteousness among a few. Persons committed to the goals of Emmaus may not currently participate in an accountability group for good reason: people move away and groups lose members; Community members cannot find a group or are between groups; groups no longer meet members' needs; schedule changes cause members to drop out; persons have a current commitment to a group of an equivalent nature.

Recognizing the validity of these reasons does not lessen commitment to and confidence in the accountability group method as a discipline of life and an effective means of grace. We honor the unique manner and timing in which the Holy Spirit brings renewal to each person's life. Guidelines for team participation emphasize the importance of accountability group involvement, erring on the side of grace and inclusion rather than law and exclusion.

- *What is the relationship between an Emmaus accountability group and other small-group formats? Is the Emmaus accountability group better?*

The unique dimension of the Emmaus accountability group is as its name indicates: *accountability*. The accountability to one another as friends in Christ for our faithfulness as disciples is a dynamic of Christian life and growth that many small-group experiences do not provide. The accountability group assumes the participant's desire to grow in grace and commitment to practice the Christian disciplines of piety, study, and action. People become part of an accountability group because they desire a life in grace, and they need help to keep walking this path. By becoming a part of an accountability group, we open ourselves to God before other people. We ask them to support us, encourage us, and hold us accountable for the promises we make about the way we want to live in relationship to Jesus Christ. We trust that this dynamic is itself a means of grace that will facilitate growth in us as new persons in Christ.

The Emmaus accountability group method is more productive than other group methods for the person who earnestly wants to live as a disciple of Jesus Christ in daily life with the support of other committed Christians. An accountability group is no better than other groups for a person whose desire is to learn more about the Bible, talk about personal problems, or pray with other people. The accountability group design does not emphasize these features, although it may include elements of each. The accountability group dynamic will help persons *follow through* on commitments to study the Bible, to pray, or to handle personal difficulties with grace.

Above all, an accountability group reinforces awareness of Christ's presence in our daily life and strengthens our commitment to practice the fundamental disciplines of a life in grace: piety, study, and action. The accountability group represents a vital means of grace—a life discipline of mutual support and accountability among persons who become companions on the journey to God through Christ by the power and guidance of the Holy Spirit.

Other group formats serve the same purpose in their own way, one being covenant discipleship groups. We appreciate and affirm persons who participate in these groups as their way of making the accountability group dynamic a part of their lives.

Organizations other than an Emmaus Community may host Journey to the Table. When that is the case, leaders encourage Journey to the Table participants to engage fully within their faith Community in small groups that provide ongoing and positive accountability. If such small groups do not exist, it makes sense for the participants and/or the supervisory team to consider the Emmaus accountability group as a model to develop Community and accountability.

The critical consideration is not whether persons may only attend an Emmaus accountability group or whether only those who have attended Emmaus make up an accountability group. The emphasis is this: Persons who want to live in grace as disciples find groups that offer support, encouragement, and accountability like that of the Emmaus accountability group.

- *Why do we follow the group card?*

The card's purpose comes in guiding the group in spiritual conversation in the manner of any natural conversation. When we come together in everyday situations, we ask one another, "How's it been going?" and "What have you been doing?" Then we may move to deeper levels of sharing, asking one another, "Are you enjoying what you are doing? What good is happening in your life? How are you fulfilling your goals in life? What issues are you struggling with?" And finally, "What are your plans for the week ahead?"

Likewise, in accountability group formats we begin by inquiring of one another, "How has your walk with the Lord been going? How have you been doing in your piety, study, and action?" Then we move to deeper levels of sharing about how we have experienced Christ's presence this week, how we succeeded and failed in our discipleship goals, what our struggles with life and the Lord are. We share our discipleship plans for the week to come. So the card intends to guide us naturally not legalistically.

The card also keeps us on task with the purpose of the group meeting. Conversing about the spiritual dimension of our lives is not easy or natural for most of us. Many weeks we would prefer to talk about anything but our piety, study, and action. So we spend thirty minutes talking about the weather or enjoying a diversion about someone's past week. We can always talk about something other than our spiritual lives. That is why we meet in an accountability group: to set aside a time and space in which we focus on our walk with the risen Lord. The card keeps us on track.

Experience has proven that faithfulness to the group card's intent produces more vital and enduring accountability groups. These groups maintain the ingredient of paying attention to one another's practice of piety, study, and action. They care about the others' walk with the Lord and their life goals and directions. Members of groups who habitually shy away from the life dimensions the group card points us toward may wonder why they go to the trouble to meet.

COMMUNITY MEETINGS OR GATHERINGS

The Community Gathering is the monthly reunion of the Emmaus Community, open to all members and their guests. Participation of all the active Emmaus Ministries is to be purposefully included in the Gathering agenda. Objectives of Gatherings are as follows:

- to make visible the Christian community—persons of various churches and denominations who unite in pursuing transformation in the calling of "one Lord, one faith, one baptism" (Eph. 4:5);

- to encourage one another to continue our walk with the Lord and to persevere in grace through the practice of piety, study, and action through membership in an accountability group and through active participation in a church;

- to inspire one another to make profound changes in our own lives and in the environments in which we live;

- to maintain relationships with other Emmaus Community members that build a vital Community of persons to support future Emmaus events; and

- to educate the Emmaus Community in the Emmaus movement, its events, and method for living in the Fourth Day.

We see the heart of the Gathering in Luke 24:33-36 after Cleopas and the other disciple's eyes are opened and they recognize Jesus as the stranger in their midst. These two disciples return within the hour to Jerusalem and find "the eleven and their companions gathered together." They share stories of how the Lord had appeared to Simon and to the two on the road and in the breaking of the bread. Even as they share, "Jesus himself stood among them."

Emmaus Community members attempt to view every day that follows their spiritual renewal event as an ongoing walk to Emmaus in the company of the risen Christ. Just as the eleven gathered together, the monthly Gathering is a time for the Community to share their Resurrection stories of how God became real to them: on the road with a friend or through a stranger, through scripture, in the breaking of the bread, and in the sharing of agape love. Through singing and prayer, small groups, Fourth Day talks, and Holy Communion, Community members share their stories and help one another recognize the risen Christ in the midst of their lives.

The two resources *Leader's Manual for Cursillos in Christianity* and *Your Fourth Day* provide additional information on the historical background of Gatherings.

Basic Components of a Gathering

An Emmaus Gathering generally consists of five or six familiar activities: singing and prayer, small-group sharing, Fourth Day witness, clergy response, Holy Communion, and Community education or making agape.

Singing and Prayer

Singing and prayer open participants to God's presence and allow all to take part as they feel led. The inspiration of music that typified the members' Emmaus Ministries events is found again in the Gathering. The Gathering also provides an opportunity to share in prayer for upcoming events and participants, for people's needs, for the church, and for the world.

Small-Group Sharing

These random groupings of three persons for a short time to respond to some question from the accountability group card or a question from the Gathering leader are often referred to as "floating" groups. This sharing helps break the ice, builds relationships beyond the usual accountability groups, and prepares participants for the evening by having them reflect briefly on their spiritual lives. During this time persons may also seek out clergy for spiritual counseling.

Fourth Day Witness

A person bears witness to God's presence in his or her life and developments in his or her walk with the risen Lord. The witness may stem from a reflection on his or her past spiritual journey, an experience of God's challenge to live more fully in holiness and service, or a recent experience in his or her walk with God: an insight from scripture and prayer, an encounter with God in daily life, a realization of the difference that being a Christian makes, a witness to the power of Christian friendships, a call to discipleship or a situation that tested faithfulness, or an experience of what the church is all about.

The style of the Fourth Day Witness is conversational; it is not a sermon, teaching, or exhortation. Nor is it an Emmaus talk or a nostalgic remembering of a person's Emmaus event. The Fourth Day Witness is a first-person sharing, peer to peer, that will cause others to reflect on God's presence and call in their own lives and will inspire them to live more fully in grace as disciples. The Fourth Day Witness comes from the heart, is thoughtful and well-prepared, and lasts ten minutes or fewer. The speaker benefits others from personal experience and stimulates listeners' reflections on their own walks with the Lord.

Sometimes those gathered may respond extemporaneously to the Fourth Day Witness's resonance with their own life stories. After a moment of silent reflection, the leader of the Gathering may ask the participants to respond aloud in the large group or form smaller groups to share.

Clergy Response

A response from the evening Clergy Director sometimes follows the Fourth Day Witness (and Community responses). It pulls together the various thoughts and highlights further connections with the gospel. This response is neither a sermon nor a prepared talk but scriptural reflection on the general theme of the Fourth Day Witness for the purpose of deepening the listeners' understanding of the connection between their lives and the story of God in scripture. The lay speaker will have shared the basic intent of the Fourth Day Witness with the Clergy Director ahead of time. The clergy response is secondary to the Fourth Day Witness and lasts no longer than ten minutes. The clergy response can also provide a transition to Holy Communion or be incorporated into a brief Holy Communion meditation.

Holy Communion

Holy Communion becomes the centerpiece of the Emmaus Gathering, just as it is central to an Emmaus Ministries event. In Holy Communion, the participants celebrate God's presence, hear again the sacred story of God's presence with us in Jesus Christ through the Holy Spirit, and symbolize their unity as brothers and sisters in Christ though they come from different churches and denominations.

Agape / Community Education

Either at the beginning or end, Gatherings become times of sharing agape in the form of food, refreshments, and good conversation among friends in the Emmaus Community. The Agape chair may combine this sharing with making agape as a Community for upcoming events by providing materials. Community leaders may promote prayer agape and pass around 72-Hour Prayer Vigil charts for upcoming events for sign-ups. Gatherings also offer a setting for Community education on aspects of the Emmaus movement, the Emmaus Ministries events, or the Fourth Day. Gatherings are a regular forum for passing on the Emmaus tradition and method from one generation of participants to the next. Even five to ten minutes of education on a particular topic can help.

Formats for a Gathering

Below are three Gathering formats. These formats reflect three variations on a common pattern. Each Community's creativity will come into play. The time frames are suggestions. Some Community Gatherings follow a strict schedule, while others have no apparent schedule or agreed-upon ending time.

Format A

7:00 p.m. Gathering together
- Refreshments and fellowship
- Opening songs and prayers
- Community Lay Director (or Gathering leader) welcomes all and introduces new Community members and guests. (This activity of welcoming and introducing is important because the Gathering may be a doorway to an Emmaus Ministries event for some and the first exposure to the Fourth Day Community for new members.)
- Introduction of clergy worship leader for the evening

7:20 p.m. Small-group sharing
- Pray the Prayer to the Holy Spirit together.
- Form groups of three; distribute new members among the groups.
- Groups focus on some aspect of their accountability group card.
- Groups close with prayer.
- Everyone is called back together with singing.

7:50 p.m. Fourth Day Witness
- Gathering leader introduces the speaker.
- Talk lasts ten minutes or less.
- Community members briefly respond to the witness.
- The Community celebrates the witness with a song.
- Clergy response makes the transition to Holy Communion.

8:10 p.m. Holy Communion
- Community prayer, open to everyone, and ending with evening Clergy Director
- Scripture reading and brief Communion meditation (or scriptural response to the theme of the Fourth Day Witness)
- Liturgy and sharing at the table of our Lord

8:45 p.m. Announcements

8:50 p.m. Fellowship, agape, and education
- More refreshments, fellowship, and singing
- Making agape for upcoming Emmaus Ministries events
- Community education

   A Community could devote this time to a presentation by members of a strong accountability group on its value for them and on what keeps their group vital and helpful. The leadership can offer an opportunity for those who want to join a group to find others with a similar interest and begin to make plans.

   Education topics could include sponsorship, the growth of the Emmaus movement, the Emmaus Community organization, the importance of prayer agape during events, or how to relate Emmaus to the local church in a positive way.

Format B

In this less-detailed format, small groups serve the same purpose as table groups on Emmaus events. The evening can also revolve around a single theme such as love or servanthood.

7:00 p.m. Gathering together; singing and prayer

7:20 p.m. Fourth Day Witness on a chosen theme (10 minutes)

7:35 p.m. Song to celebrate the witness

7:40 p.m. Clergy response to relate theme to scripture without upstaging the Fourth Day Witness (5–7 minutes)

7:50 p.m. Small groups for persons to relate personally to the Fourth Day Witness and for clergy response; the sharing may center around these questions:
What was said that caught your attention? Why?
How does this speak to your life and how?

8:05 p.m. Singing, prayer, and concerns; announcements

Emmaus Ministries Community Manual

8:20 p.m.   Holy Communion

8:45 p.m.   Fellowship, agape, and education

Format C

The Community leadership may choose to incorporate the main elements of the Gathering into the service of Holy Communion. Small groups of three may share together during the opening portions of the service and/or in response to the Fourth Day Witness, which may replace the sermon. The Clergy Director provides a transition from the Fourth Day Witness to the remainder of the liturgy of Holy Communion in the form of a brief response to the talk or a brief Communion meditation. Special music may be interspersed throughout the service. Refreshments, announcements, the making of agape, and Community education take their place before or after the service.

More Ideas for Gatherings

- Have an active Gathering chair who plans the evening.

- Communities may benefit by asking team members and participants from the most recent Community-sponsored Emmaus events to lead the subsequent Gathering. Then the whole Community benefits from the overflow of the Spirit: The Community meets some of the new Community members, and leadership for several Gatherings each year is provided.

- For Emmaus ministries not currently offered by the Community (such as Chrysalis, Face to Face), consider asking persons from the Community's geographical area who participated elsewhere in one of those ministry events to provide the leadership for one Emmaus Gathering annually. For example, have the area youth who attended Chrysalis lead the entire Gathering according to the Community's format. This gives the Emmaus Community exposure to other Emmaus opportunities and ensures that participants of all Emmaus ministries feel like part of the local community.

- Gatherings can include agape-making parties in preparation for upcoming events.

- Gatherings can combine with a Candlelight service in the months that coincide with an Emmaus event. In these instances, guests may not attend the Gatherings.

- Providing childcare for Gatherings frees those with youngsters to participate.

- People will come to Gatherings as long as they can relate person-to-person with those present, feel a part of what is happening, and find their faith rekindled through the witness of friends. People will stop coming to Gatherings that become spectator events, routine, or begin to resemble a typical Sunday morning worship service.

- Beginning with lengthy business proceedings and announcements will weigh down the Gatherings. Conducting Emmaus business is the work of the Board of Directors. The Gatherings serve a different purpose: to celebrate God's presence and to inspire one another to persevere in grace. Limit business matters to announcements during this time.

- Emmaus Communities that cover a large geographical area or include several metropolitan areas can cultivate the Emmaus movement by establishing regular local Gatherings, with area-wide Gatherings being held occasionally or annually.

- Emmaus Communities are encouraged to contact other Emmaus Communities to get ideas for improving attendance at Gatherings.

EMMAUS AND CHURCH PARTNERSHIP

The sole purpose of the Emmaus movement is to strengthen disciples within the ministry of individual congregations. Emmaus, in partnership with the church, inspires leaders to become more effective and intentional in their ministry. Emmaus is neither competitive with nor a substitute for your own church. Although The Walk to Emmaus is a unique and powerful instrument through which faithful people are renewed and inspired, it cannot provide the well-rounded programs that an individual congregation offers, such as education, evangelism, missions, and stewardships. In short, Emmaus does not intend to become anyone's "new church." However, Emmaus does have a unique role in the church's task of nurturing strong, committed disciples who compassionately serve Christ in the world. The unique role of The Walk to Emmaus is spiritual renewal.
—*Day Four: The Pilgrim's Continued Journey*

Emmaus Is for the Church

Participants can maximize the benefit of the Emmaus movement and minimize problems by staying focused on its purpose in relation to the church. Eager Emmaus Ministries participants who desire spiritual growth sometimes ask, "What's next after Emmaus?" The best and truest answer is, "Your church!" Emmaus is not simply another in a series of retreats for individuals. Rather, Emmaus provides a means by which Christians reclaim their Christian heritage with enthusiasm and return to their churches with new vision and commitment. As indicated in *Coming Down from the Mountain: Returning to Your Congregation*, Emmaus comes from the church, and Emmaus returns to the church. What follows is a potpourri of images, ideas, and suggestions for making the most of the relationship between Emmaus and the church.

Emmaus as a "Complementary Crop"

The image of *complementary planting* depicts the proper relationship between Emmaus and the church. This term refers to the practice of planting particular plants with special qualities alongside the primary crop in order to enhance the productivity of the primary crop. For instance, marigolds repel harmful insects and can benefit other crops, such as tomatoes, simply by their presence around the borders of the garden. But if tomato gardeners get carried away with the "marigold experience"—looking at beautiful marigolds, caring for marigolds, and making marigolds productive for their own sake—they would not necessarily succeed as tomato gardeners. Marigolds as a complementary crop are not judged for their beauty and productivity but for the resulting productivity of the tomatoes.

Emmaus is a complementary crop in relation to the church. Though people may have beautiful, life-changing experiences on Emmaus Ministries events, the movement does not fulfill its mission by producing Emmaus experiences. The Emmaus movement's mission is to complement the ministry of area churches and to strengthen the local Christian community. Communities evaluate the success of the Emmaus movement in this broader understanding.

Emmaus as "Leaven in the Loaf"

Jesus gives us a way of viewing God's renewal and our participation in the spiritual-renewal process. Jesus says the change God brings about "is like yeast that a woman took and mixed in with three measures of flour until all of it was leavened" (Luke 13:21). The amount of leaven seems insignificant in comparison to the whole, but it transforms the three measures of flour by giving up its identity as leaven and releasing its qualities within the whole. The leaven's work is hidden and patient. The yeast does not remain distinctive but blends in and betters what is already there.

The Emmaus movement is intended to be such a leavening influence in the life of the church. Just as leaven does not work by turning all the flour into leaven, renewal does not require getting everyone in a church to go to Emmaus. *Renewal comes, not by getting the whole church into Emmaus, but by getting the gifts of Emmaus into the church.* Not all, or even most, church members will ever participate in Emmaus Ministries events; this is not a realistic strategy for renewal in most churches. But the quiet, persevering influence of a few leaders and members who return to their congregations with a renewed spirit and vision can transform and spread. Those who participate in Emmaus Ministries accept the challenge of finding creative ways to involve themselves in the life of the church and to share the gifts they have received—not as "Emmaus-ites" but as Christians and members of Christ's body.

There Is Nothing Secret about Emmaus

Emmaus Ministries participants can harm the unity of the church by acting as though Emmaus involves secrecy, like a lodge or a mystery cult. The greatest obstacle to a graceful relationship between Emmaus and the church over the years has been the perceived sense of secrecy. Secrets create barriers; they bind together those "in the know" and separate them from those who do not know. Christians share in a mystery now revealed to all: "the mystery that has been hidden throughout the ages and generations but has now been revealed . . . the riches of the glory of this mystery, which is Christ in you, the hope of glory" (Col. 1:26-27).

Nothing about Emmaus is secret. Sponsors may mention Candlelight, personal agape letters, and the Community's presence at the Closing when explaining Emmaus to a prospective participant. The hope is that participants will experience these elements afresh as surprises and as gifts. Even when anticipated, little is lost when persons encounter the love these special elements of the event communicate. When asked a specific question, Emmaus Community members give an honest answer.

Emmaus Community members hurt the movement when they tell people, "Well, I can't tell you what happens." This is not true. We may have trouble putting into words the experience of an Emmaus Ministries event, and we can say more than our friends are interested in hearing. Nevertheless, the Emmaus event contains objective ingredients that members can share with prospective participants. The brochure, "The Upper Room Walk to Emmaus—For the Development of Christian Leaders" and the book *What Is Emmaus?* describe these objective ingredients openly: talks, discussion groups, meaningful services of prayer and Holy Communion, and acts of love by a support Community.

The Proper Expression of "Emmaus Love"

Emmaus Community members also harm the unity of the church by appearing to prefer to congregate with those who have been through Emmaus. God gives us *Christian* love on the weekend, not *Emmaus* love. Emmaus members share the love they received on their Emmaus event with everyone. Most Community members simply require awareness of these potential problems to avoid them. Others require reminders and shepherding in this regard. Conscious disregard for the negative effects of action in the congregation reflects selfishness and arrogance. Emmaus members use the gifts they have received through Emmaus for the building of the body and heed Paul's admonition: "Take care that this liberty of yours does not somehow become a stumbling block" (1 Cor. 8:9). A good resource for helping participants return to their congregations is *Coming Down from the Mountain.*

Communicate Openly with the Church

Openness and communication can enhance the partnership between Emmaus and the participants' churches. Below are some helpful practices. The Community Clergy Director can assist with these practices. Often pastors will listen more readily to other pastors.

- Communicate Emmaus Ministries activities on church calendars. Include the dates of upcoming Emmaus events on church and denominational calendars. Make it clear in general publicity that persons desiring to go on a Walk to Emmaus or Chrysalis event require a sponsor. Churches can publish times and meeting places of accountability groups alongside other activities and meetings. This listing provides further evidence for the open nature of Emmaus and the integration of Emmaus with the total program of spirituality offered by a congregation. Even members who have not attended an Emmaus Ministries event can participate in accountability groups and Gatherings. Church members who come to Community Gatherings feel encouraged when members of their congregation sit with them and make them feel welcome. Inviting people to Gatherings or to be part of an accountability group can be a step toward sponsoring them.

- Make Emmaus Ministries application forms, educational materials, and articles about Emmaus Ministries visibly available to the entire congregation. This offering helps emphasize that Emmaus is not a by-invitation-only, secret organization.

- Identify in church communications the participants who have recently returned from an Emmaus Ministries event, as well as the team members who served. This identification encourages church members to inquire about Emmaus and get more information and also affirms those who have attended.

- Report on Emmaus to the denominational leaders. Emmaus is part of the church and views itself as accountable for the quality of its impact on the church and on people. So take the initiative to report on Emmaus to church leaders or annual church meetings of denominations affected by Emmaus. Seek organizational links or reporting channels with church leaders or church structures. Such communication helps Emmaus leadership listen to and speak to the church while not threatening the autonomy of the Emmaus Board to lead the Emmaus movement. Such connections also help church leaders feel that Emmaus represents a valuable part of the body of Christ that is accessible and responsible.

- Present Emmaus Ministries to clergy in forums. Hold Emmaus introductory meetings once a year for clergy who have not participated in an Emmaus event, led by clergy who have participated. Emphasize the aims, the actual results in many people's lives, and the importance of solid clergy leadership in Emmaus for the sake of the church. Be open and nondefensive in response to questions and criticism. The video titled *An Introduction to The Walk to Emmaus* and the book titled *What Is Emmaus?* are excellent resources for these forums. The video can be shown, and copies of the book can be distributed.

- Openly introduce Emmaus to groups in churches. Hold Emmaus introductory meetings in churches that already have a few participants and pastoral support for Emmaus. Be prepared to take steps toward sponsoring persons who show interest. Publicly invite everyone who is interested to come and be intentional about personally inviting persons you want to sponsor. The video and book mentioned above are useful resources for these meetings.

- Encourage pastors to choose both Emmaus and non-Emmaus laity when providing lay readers, lay liturgists, or devotional leaders for church worship and meetings.

- Host occasional meetings of members from your congregation who have experienced Emmaus to discuss the role of Emmaus in the local church, to remind and educate them about how best to share about Emmaus, and to consider who may be ready to attend the next Emmaus Ministries event. Such meetings also provide a good time to review the importance of those in Emmaus participating in the life of the congregation and to review material from the book *Day Four: The Pilgrim's Continued Journey*.

- Write a letter to pastors of recent Emmaus Ministries participants to inform them of their members' participation, to interpret Emmaus, and to invite them to shepherd and employ the participants wisely after their Emmaus Ministries events. See the sample letter in the Sample Letters and Handouts section of this manual.

Emmaus Ministries as Part of the Church's Total Discipleship Program

- Emphasize the importance of spiritual formation and the need for spiritual growth for all persons throughout their life journey. Church leadership can introduce Emmaus as one valuable option for youth and adult spiritual growth without suggesting that Emmaus provides all the spiritual formation necessary for people in one milestone experience.

- Use Emmaus as part of a total program of spiritual formation or spiritual growth. Don't let it become the congregation's only source of leadership development or spiritual growth. Let Emmaus Ministries be among choices that may include intercessory prayer groups, sharing groups, Bible study groups, or covenant discipleship groups. The formation of an Upper Room Covenant Prayer Group, a local chapter of the Disciplined Order of Christ, and a healing and wholeness ministry suggests a variety of methods for reclaiming our spiritual heritage. These methods also provide additional opportunities for members who are returning from Emmaus. A church will offer Emmaus as one avenue among many, not the only way.

- Build on the interest in spiritual growth that Emmaus inspires among church members by planning spiritual life opportunities for the whole congregation. Schedule additional experiences for spiritual life planning, education, and retreat either away from or at your local church for all church members. Provide a selection of short-term spiritual growth opportunities on a regular basis. Make it clear that these spiritual growth endeavors are not part of or sponsored by Emmaus. Encourage accountable discipleship as a long-term theme for the whole church. Emmaus participants with experience in accountability groups may initiate small-group efforts such as covenant discipleship or intercessory prayer groups in the congregation.

- Seek more frequent opportunities for church members to celebrate Holy Communion.

- Pray for and support the pastors. At one church, Emmaus participants pray for the pastor during his sermon just as they pray for speakers during an Emmaus event. The aim of such prayer is not narrowly aimed at persuading the pastor to participate in Emmaus but at supporting the pastor in guiding the church's ministry. Pastors can become the loneliest persons in the congregation when they work without a sense of support. Emmaus participants go out of their way to relate to pastors as friends and partners in ministry.

- Take advantage of the many spiritual growth options provided by Upper Room Ministries. Find a number of such ideas for individuals, groups, and the congregation on the Upper Room Ministries website *upperroom.org*.

- Assist the Emmaus Ministries participants in returning to the local church. The book *Coming Down from the Mountain: Returning to Your Congregation* is a valuable tool. This book will help the participant, the sponsor, and the pastor.

SECTION 7— GENERAL REMINDERS

It would be impractical to include information about every contingency, concern, or possible happening in The Upper Room Emmaus Ministries programs. This section explains and clarifies some issues that have been known to arise.

CHURCH DIVERSITY

Each Community intentionally works to ensure a diverse representation of churches on each event. The event's Conference Room Team evidences this diversity as well as an event's participants. The Upper Room Emmaus model values diversity and includes representation from various denominations, as well as nondenominational and different churches within denominations.

These aspects of diversity are essential for the participants so they will understand and appreciate the ecumenicity of the Emmaus program. The diversity of the team members helps participants realize that several church "types" lead the Emmaus experience. Diversity among the participants facilitates each participant's having his or her own experience and helps the Community develop its diversity, in accordance with the Emmaus model.

Conference Room Team

Communities ensure that members of one church do not constitute a large proportion of the Conference Room Team. A convenient guideline considers the number of participant tables in the conference room to determine the maximum number of people from one church to be on the Conference Room Team; this generally results in no more than one third of the lay Conference Room Team members being from the same church.

Another guideline involves distributing team members from one church among the tables so that leadership at each table (Table Leaders, Assistant Table Leaders, adult Table Leaders, youth Table Leaders) represents various churches.

The clergy team members also reflect church, denominational, and theological diversity.

Ethnic diversity is a significant consideration for the Conference Room Team, conveying a powerful message to the participants: God's equal love transcends ethnic definitions, and God shows no partiality.

The Community Board of Directors bears the responsibility for assuring Conference Room Team diversity. The board establishes the team diversity policy aspects, and the Team Selection Committee carries them out.

Event Participants

For a given event, limiting the number of participants from one church can free them to have their own experience of the event and helps the Community develop its diversity, which is part of The Upper Room Emmaus Ministries model. This limit may not apply to a Journey to the Table or Face to Face ministry event, which may be hosted by or held for a specific organization or faith Community.

For Walk to Emmaus and Chrysalis events, limit the number of participants from one church to the number of participant tables in the conference room. Participants from the same church sit at different tables.

The Community Board of Directors takes responsibility for assuring diversity among participants of its ministries. The board establishes the participant diversity policy aspects, and the Registrar carries them out. A Community that remains alert to the policy and the need for church diversity will not expend all its energy to invite many people from one church to attend a particular event. The Registrar records the participants' church affiliations, and the person preparing the table assignments has that information.

PARTICIPANTS LEAVING BEFORE COMPLETING THE EVENT

Unfortunate circumstances sometimes arise in which a participant has to withdraw before completion of an event. Three such circumstances have been acknowledged: sickness, medical emergency, and family emergency. The timing of a participant's departure directly impacts that participant's status with the event and the Emmaus Community.

Departure prior to the Candlelight service

The Community does not consider these individuals as Fourth Day members of the Emmaus movement and encourages them to attend a future event in its entirety. The personal agape letters are returned to the sponsor to hold for a later event.

Departure after the completion of the Candlelight service

The Community considers these individuals as Fourth Day members of the Emmaus movement; that is, they qualify to serve on future Emmaus teams or in support roles. They receive their participant cross and their agape letters. It helps to have their Table Leader meet with them at a later time to give a synopsis of the activities and elements they missed.

LEANING INTO THE FOURTH DAY

Like the event of Jesus' transfiguration, each Emmaus event is designed and experienced with a view of what comes next. Mark 9:2 records that Jesus led Peter, James, and John "up a high mountain apart, by themselves"; there they beheld his glory. Jesus does not lead his three friends to that mountaintop experience so they will stay on the mountain but to increase their faith and vision for the difficult journey that lay ahead—the journey to the cross. Similarly, for every Emmaus Ministries event, we pray that the Holy Spirit will lead the participants to the high mountain of spiritual awareness, but we do not want them to stay there. The aim of Emmaus is to increase participants' vision and faith for the journey that lies ahead—the rest of their lives. If the leaders of an event do not keep an eye on the real context for Christian living—the valley below and the uneven journey with Jesus that lies ahead—then the Emmaus experience can become an end in itself and an obstacle to authentic faith for living.

Each part of an Emmaus event leans into the next, and the entire event leans into the Fourth Day. The event's early reflections and talks emphasize God and God's initiative of grace and lean into the next part's focus on a response to grace. The activities that emphasize a response to the grace of Jesus Christ begin to lean into a focus on the Christian community in action during and after Candlelight. In Candlelight, the participants experience the outreach of the Christian community on their behalf and recommit their lives as disciples in that community. The event's final activities focus on the community of the Holy Spirit being Christ in the world and lean into the first day after the event and every Fourth Day thereafter.

Emmaus attempts to strengthen participants for living their Fourth Day. In fact, people reach the goal of Emmaus only in the Fourth Day. Participants clearly need to understand this aspect on the final day of the event. All Emmaus Ministries events are designed to be led with a Fourth Day perspective.

Communities and teams sometimes unconsciously emphasize the powerful events of "dying moments" Communion and Candlelight, possibly diminishing the impact and effectiveness of later Fourth Day messages about accountability groups, church renewal, and participant involvement in the Emmaus Community.

Each experience on an Emmaus event, while critical, remains in perspective with God's guidance of the participants through the total experience of the event. The Fourth Day for the Emmaus Community is not simply time between events to prepare for more events but time to work as Christian disciples and to support one another as active Christians in the church and everyday environments. The arena of lasting transformation is not a singular event but daily life in the world with God. What shapes lives most in the long run is not a single mountaintop experience but the resulting relationships with other Christians who decide to meet, pray, study, and support one another's struggle to live lives of faith, hope, and love.

KEEPING THE SCHEDULE

Each step along the way carries significance on any Emmaus Ministries event. The schedule, like a trusted map, guides the leaders and the team alike and assures them that they are on the same road as every event held around the world . . . no matter who may be in the driver's seat.

The schedule allows time for each step, which assures the participants enough time to experience the whole event. When leaders reallocate time, they may be making a value judgment about which parts of the event are more important on the basis of their own experience and needs. Granting more time for the participants to experience one part of the journey may mean rushing past another meaningful part for participants with different needs. The schedule keeps the participants moving at a reasonable pace and balances their use of time for the sake of the whole experience.

The schedule also takes into account the need for participants to take breaks and to rest. Emmaus Ministries events are not marathons or long-distance marches with the aim of wearing down the participants until they break. Leaders with this intention do not represent faith in the power of God's presence in people's lives, nor do they respect the participants' dignity. Further, they do a disservice to the Emmaus movement. An Emmaus event has a full agenda, is intense at points, and can be emotionally tiring even *without* the well-intentioned but misguided help of leaders who want to stretch it out further. Leaders respect the participants' need for occasional unstructured time and work to protect the allotted time for breaks, recreation, reflection, and rest so the participants remain alert and refreshed.

The schedule serves as a guide, a discipline, and a goal. The event works best when leaders adhere to the schedule. Yet those who try to maintain a rigid schedule down to the minute will experience frustration and may also frustrate the participants.

While the event leaders need to be firm about the schedule, they maintain enough flexibility that the participants do not feel pressured and regimented. Sometimes the participants may require a few more minutes to discuss a particular talk; at other times, they may need less time and will sit idle and bored unless leaders notice and respond. A large group of participants will require more time for Communion, sharing with the entire group, and moving from place to place. Sometimes special needs arise that command the attention of team members and delay the event. In these cases, the leadership calls upon the event clergy team leaders to fulfill their pastoral role rather than hold up the event indefinitely.

Ringing a bell is a helpful way to shift attention to the next step of the schedule. The participants' response time to the bell tends to become slower as the event progresses. Some simply stop hearing the bell. During team meetings, remind the team members to encourage promptness by example and to echo to persons around them the call to the conference room when the bell rings.

Sensitivity of the event leadership to the needs of the moment allows for wise adjustments to the schedule. If the event falls behind schedule, the event leader looks ahead for places to save time while protecting necessary scheduled blocks of time, such as the time to read individual agape letters and the scheduled long break. If the event runs ahead of schedule, the leaders avoid imposing more structured activity on the participants. The event leader can give the participants more free time to be alone, to visit informally and develop relationships, to sing, or to further discuss and consider responses to the talks.

TONE OF EACH PART OF THE EVENT AND TEAM DISPOSITION

Since the team members already know one another well and have journeyed far together as a Community, they will need to tone down their natural exuberance and enjoyment of being together to a level that the participants find comfortable. Let the participants get to know one another gradually and give them the freedom to move at their own pace. The participants need space to reflect on what is happening and to begin to trust the leaders. As the event progresses and the Spirit begins to move, team members express sensitivity to the developing sense of community by encouraging a deeper level of sharing and outward support for one another. Always, the team members set the tone by participating in a natural, joyful, and wholehearted manner, thus exhibiting the qualities of authentic piety.

Paying attention to the teams' tone involves perceiving the time it takes to establish relationships and develop trust, avoiding aggressive Christian behavior on the part of the team, and cooperating with the initiative of the Holy Spirit in fostering spiritual community among the participants. Team members avoid contriving moods or manipulating the emotional atmosphere. They are not actors who dramatize the change from a cool and distant disposition at the start of the event to a warm and joyous disposition at the end. The design of an Emmaus event provides an environment in which the participants can authentically experience God's gift of life together in Christ. Because the leaders trust Christ to be present on the Emmaus event, they need not imitate or fabricate gifts of the event—only receive and share.

DISTRIBUTION OF AGAPE IN EMMAUS

The Emmaus Ministries model has a rationale for distributing agape during an event and for distributing the personal agape letters last. As the event unfolds, the agape becomes progressively personal. A wave of agape love that surprisingly intensifies during the unfolding event washes over the participants. Early in the event, the introduction of general agape communicates God's love for everyone primarily through Community prayer and sacrifice. Attention remains focused on the Community letters and the event Prayer Vigil. Next, the participants become especially aware of table agape. Table agape, while the same for everyone, shows up as a gift for each person, reflecting the fact that God loves us all the same but cares for each of us individually. Near the end of the event, the agape letters from family and friends communicate God's love for each participant in personal ways through relationships that are unique and unrepeatable.

Other reasons exist for waiting until near the end of the event to distribute the individual agape letters. The letters are part of the end-of-event reentry process. They come at a time when the participants feel the event is closing and the giving has surely ended. The letters show the participants that, though they may be tired and the event is almost over, God is not finished loving them and will continue to do so through the people in their lives. The letters prepare them to return with gratitude to a world with people who appreciate and provide support for them. The letters also serve as examples of Christian action as the participants are sent forth to share with others the grace they have received. The personal letters enrich the final part of the event and make personal the summary message of being the church wherever participants find themselves, which is the goal of Emmaus Ministries.

Above all, the distribution of the individual agape letters near the event's end supports the concept of the event as a time set apart from usual patterns and relationships in which the participants can sort out and reestablish their relationship with God. At the start of the event, the participants just begin to let go of their focus on relationships back home and to turn their attention to a deeper relationship with God. Early on, some may struggle as they question why they are there, learn the rhythm of the event, and begin to get a fresh perspective on their lives.

Particularly for the cloistered events of the Walk to Emmaus and Chrysalis, team members may have an unfounded fear that participants will leave early unless they are opened up emotionally by receiving their personal letters early in the event. The intent of the letters is not to improve participants' feelings about the Emmaus event or to influence them to stay for the duration. The letters are part of the progression of agape, moving from general to specific and then to personal.

Likewise, at other times during the course of the event, receiving personal letters would shift the focus and likely crowd an already full and emotionally charged schedule with more. Letters from loved ones at any time will be a good experience and provide a lift, but they do not necessarily serve the design of the Emmaus event. Generating an emotional high or a particular atmosphere for the participants' community is not the purpose of the personal letters. The letters help the participants realize that they are loved, not only in the event Community, but by people in the world to which they are returning.

THE LEARNING PROCESS

The methodology of talk, silence, and discussion (and, for The Walk to Emmaus and Chrysalis, summaries, representations, and sharing in the evening) is a learning process integral to Emmaus that makes it possible for everyone to participate. The silence provides time for everyone to meditate on the content of the message before talking about it during the discussion time. Creating representations can bring out the best in both the talkers and the doers—those more attuned to concepts and those more attuned to images—and can encourage each to learn through the strengths of the other. Learning not only results from new rational understandings but from changes in people's operating images of themselves, life, and God. The summary representation time provides an opportunity for participants to invent their own images for holding and appropriating the truth they receive on their Emmaus events.

For The Walk to Emmaus and Chrysalis, requiring each table to present joint summaries and posters, skits, or songs in the evening challenges the participants to work together on common tasks and to become a Community of persons who respect one another's gifts and uniquenesses. Sharing all summaries and the representations at once in the evening provides a way to reinforce the main ideas and images of the whole day's message, while having fun as an entire Community. The total process intends to facilitate both informational and formational learning, to stimulate rich dialogue and interaction, and to foster development of relationships at the tables around a common task.

HONORING THE COMMUNITY-BUILDING PROCESS

Over the course of the Emmaus event, the many individuals in the conference room—team and participants alike—become a community of faith. Because the Holy Spirit needs the space and time to build the community and to weave the participants together in love, the participants are generally cloistered for the duration of the event. The participants enjoy freedom of expression, openness, and intimacy as they grow in their trust, love, and understanding of one another by the grace of God. This community experience offers a glimpse of the abundant life Christ came to give and a vision of what the church is meant to be.

To preserve the cloistered atmosphere of the experience, people other than the Conference Room Team have no contact with the participants during the event. The obvious exceptions to this rule are the parts of the event that include members of the Emmaus Community: Candlelight, meal servers, etc. Even in these instances, the Community members are present only in their servant roles to do their part; they do not enter into casual relationship with the participants. Community members do not enter the conference room to hear a talk or to mix with the participants. Leaders remind the team members and participants ahead of time that no talks, table dialogues, or other parts of the event will be recorded. Boards will ensure that no part of the event experience will be videotaped, electronically recorded, or photographed. Talks will not be broadcast outside the conference room.

BAPTISM AND THE EMMAUS EVENT

No one performs baptisms during Emmaus Ministries events. Baptism for youth and adults is a sign of God's unconditional love and the individual's conscious acceptance of his or her membership in the body of Christ as it finds expression through some specific congregation or denomination. Emmaus is not a church or a denomination. It complements and supports, not replaces, ongoing church ministries in helping persons grow as disciples. If persons were baptized on Emmaus events, then the Emmaus Community would function as a church body to which Christians belong; the event clergy team leader would play a role that belongs to a participant's pastor.

When participants seek baptism on an Emmaus event, the event clergy team leader counsels with them about the affirmation of faith they desire to make, helps them decide how best to act on it after the Emmaus event, and supports them in doing so. If the request for baptism surfaces as a common issue in a Community, it raises a question about the quality of the Community's sponsorship. Are sponsors inviting active Christians to enhance their spiritual formation (which is the purpose of Emmaus), or are they sponsoring non-Christians for their conversion?

CELEBRATION OF HOLY COMMUNION

While leadership may conduct Communion services during Emmaus Ministries events in creative ways, the ecumenical mission of Emmaus requires certain basic elements. At a minimum, the event clergy team leader consecrates the bread and cup, reciting the words of institution from the liturgy of Holy Communion. He or she also presents the table as open to all who seek new life in Christ, welcoming all who come forward to partake of the elements or (in the case of persons who choose not to partake in accordance with their church's guidelines) to receive a blessing.

While minimal elements are essential, event clergy team leaders are encouraged to use the entire liturgy of Holy Communion when possible, especially "The Great Thanksgiving," which includes the traditional words of institution. "The Great Thanksgiving" tells the sacred story of God's action in history through the people of God, through Jesus Christ, and through the church. It retells the story of Jesus' last supper with his disciples in the upper room and of Christ's continuing presence with us through the work of the Holy Spirit. Through regular participation in the Communion liturgy, with its telling and retelling of the story of God's action through Jesus Christ, participants learn to love the story and to make its truth part of their lives. For the Chrysalis ministry, mime Communion is, in fact, a powerful dramatization of that sacred story of God's love expressed through Jesus' birth and ministry, death and resurrection.

Event clergy team leaders bear in mind that Emmaus intends to infuse the sacrament of Holy Communion with fresh life and meaning, not only for the Emmaus event, but also for participants' ongoing life in their churches. They do no limit participants' experiences of Holy Communion to abbreviated and rare approaches to the sacrament. Therefore, the *Worship Booklet* includes *the* entire liturgy for use on the event.

BEING SLAIN IN THE SPIRIT AND OTHER PHENOMENA

Emmaus Ministries programs focus on foundational features of Christian faith with the goal of living life in grace. Being "slain in the Spirit" and other extraordinary occurrences are not essential to what The Upper Room Emmaus Ministries programs consider foundational to faith and life in Christ.

This stance does not mean that being slain in the Spirit is not meaningful, valuable, or real in some people's Christian experience. It is simply not foundational, either in scripture, tradition, or the mainstream experience of the church. Many other experiences and expressions of faith are meaningful to some but not foundational: mysticism, intentional Christian communities, speaking in tongues, casting out evil spirits, and specific stances on social issues such as abortion or nuclear war. These important concerns do find expression in the church through appropriate means. But an Emmaus Ministries event is not one of those means. These expressions of faith belong to other programs, times, and places.

Emmaus does not equip its team members to provide support to those who are slain in the Spirit. Nor can most pastors and churches provide support for persons after the fact. The only support comes from the persons who guided them into this experience to begin with, persons who do not represent Emmaus in doing so. In some groups and churches such experiences are common, and teaching accompanies these experiences; these are supportive places for being slain in the Spirit. But Emmaus offers no teaching, no context, no follow-up for this experience. Guiding individuals into these experiences on an Emmaus event is irresponsible and a disservice to the participants, Emmaus, and the church.

When team leaders agree to serve, they serve within the structures and guidelines of The Upper Room Emmaus Ministries programs. This is not their event to shape as they please. The team leaders also ensure that team members agree to serve within those boundaries. Those who do not honor this commitment need not be asked to serve again or at least not until Emmaus Community leaders feel confident about their commitment.

If people begin to identify Emmaus Ministries with a narrow religious agenda and segment of the church, that identification weakens the support of the mainstream church community and threatens the viability of the local program. When respected local church leaders communicate to The Upper Room Emmaus Ministries Office that they cannot support the quality and theological bent of a local Emmaus ministry, then The Upper Room Emmaus Ministries Office will require improvement as a condition for Emmaus to continue in that locale. The Upper Room allows use of Emmaus Ministries programs in a locale assuming the local churches and their leaders support the programs' general value for their members and their churches' ministries to them.

"DECOLORES" IN EMMAUS EVENTS

The song "DeColores" is a long-standing tradition in Cursillo and other three-day movement programs. Walk to Emmaus events uses the song "DeColores" for traveling music, and the phrase "DeColores!" concludes most talks. Although not a requirement for Chrysalis, Journey to the Table, or Face to Face events, having the Music Director teach the song can connect participants of those events with this common tradition in Emmaus and other similar three-day movements.

The words *de colores* mean "of colors" and refer to the diverse beauty of God's creation, particularly people. People who had experienced a three-day short course in Christianity wanted to express their joy about God's love in a musical way so they wrote the song text. The words are sung to an old folk tune from Majorca, Spain. When Music Directors teach "DeColores," they also explain the significance and meaning behind the song.

BALANCING LEADERSHIP OF CHRYSALIS EVENTS WITH YOUNG PEOPLE

Adult leaders initiate, plan, and conduct Chrysalis events, working cooperatively with young people who have completed a weekend. A Chrysalis event requires adult leadership in all dimensions of the program, as defined in the manuals. During a Chrysalis event, young people develop leadership skills by working side by side with adults, not by taking primary responsibility for the event.

Communities balance adult leadership with youth leadership wherever possible. Chrysalis event teams are a wonderful opportunity for young people to step out as leaders among their peers, to be visible and vocal about their faith, and to share responsibility for a significant event in people's lives. Young team members add qualities to the Chrysalis experience that adults cannot provide. After choosing youth leaders, give them genuine, not token, assignments. Provide them opportunities to appear in front of the group whenever possible so participants see them as true partners in leadership.

At the same time, the leadership of young people among their peers needs a balance with effective adult leadership that offers participants the stability, leadership experience, and maturity of adults. While keeping in mind team members' growth when making assignments, the leadership has as its main focus the participants' experience.

PARENTAL PARTICIPATION IN CHRYSALIS

Chrysalis encourages but does not require parental presence and support at selected times during the event. All parents—whether or not they have attended a Walk to Emmaus—are welcome to attend Send-Off and Closing. Candlelight, an event intended for Emmaus Communities, includes only those parents who have previously attended Chrysalis, The Walk to Emmaus, or a comparable three-day experience.

Send-Off

Send-Off precedes the beginning of the time apart with God; parents and guardians are welcome. Send-Off gives parents and the Community an opportunity to support the young people through their presence and their prayers. Parents' presence may be more appropriate in some families than others. Sponsors help non-Emmaus parents decide about their participation and make sure the young people they sponsor know that some parents will be present at Send-Off while others are not.

The presence of parents who have not attended Emmaus means Chrysalis leaders review their approaches to Send-Off to ensure they are appropriate and helpful. For example, does the exuberance of Send-Off create unnecessary anxiety in some parents and youthful participants? Are the music and language unique to "insiders" of the Emmaus experiences but a turn-off to "outsiders"? Some Emmaus Communities have toned down their Chrysalis event Send-Off in an effort to make it more inclusive and assuring.

Parents' Meeting

Some Emmaus Communities incorporate a Parents' Meeting into the Chrysalis event schedule. Others hold a meeting before the event. The purpose of the meeting is to discuss the purpose and nature of the Chrysalis ministry, common participant responses to the event, and ways parents can support their young persons afterward.

Closing

Parents are welcome to attend Closing because it follows the emergence of participants from their time apart. Closing is the participants' first chance to share their experience, as well as an opportunity for the Emmaus Community and parents to hear and celebrate what has happened for the young people by the grace of God. Parents' presence at Closing signals their support and interest in the young persons' relationship with God. It also helps parents understand the nature of the young people's experience and how they can facilitate their youth's return to the world.

Sponsors help parents decide whether or not to attend their son's or daughter's Closing. Some parents do not attend out of a desire to give their youth space from parental expectations. Sponsors need to make sure that young persons they have sponsored understand why their parents might not have been present and to make it clear that parents were welcome but not expected.

Closings can be good experiences for non-Emmaus parents, as long as the leaders follow the agenda and stay focused on the young people's responses. Closings become negative for outsiders when leaders slip into emotionalism, extended praise of the team, glorification of the Chrysalis ministry program, off-centered and simplistic theology, charismatic worship, and unrealistic views of the changes participants have undergone.

Chrysalis event leaders can elicit parents' support by relating openly to them during the Closing: for instance, by thanking them for the opportunity to work with their young people. They can praise parents for helping strengthen their youth's spiritual foundations through the church and by allowing them to participate in this time apart. In some Emmaus Communities, leaders also offer general words of advice to parents about their sons' and daughters' return.

Candlelight

Sometimes sponsors, in an effort to enhance the benefit of a Chrysalis event for young persons and their parents, want to invite parents who have not attended an Emmaus event to Candlelight. Other times, parents know about the Candlelight service and wish to participate. Their attendance is inappropriate for many reasons:

- *An invitation to all parents to participate in Candlelight is inconsistent with the Chrysalis ministry model.* Candlelight is an event internal to the experience and to Emmaus Communities. The gathered Community of those who have previously shared an Emmaus experience supports Candlelight. These people understand how their presence in this service prepares the participants for the period of prayer and commitment that follows. Parents who have not attended an Emmaus event do not understand the context of this service in the experience.

- *The appearance of all parents is out of sync with the flow of the event.* Midway through the event, Chrysalis focuses on the content of the new life based on a relationship with God in Christ. This relationship with God then becomes the foundation for renewed relationships with parents, friends, church, and society after the Chrysalis experience—the focus of the last day. Thus, all parents are encouraged to participate in Closing on the last day of the event. Of course, parents who have previously attended an Emmaus event participate in Candlelight if they wish, but they do so as members of the Emmaus Community, knowing that they hold a candle for their own youth and for every participant.

- *An open invitation to all parents to participate often translates into expectation from sponsors, youth, and the parents themselves that parents who care will participate.* Sponsors can deal with the presence or absence of parents at Send-Off and Closing. But how will they explain the presence of some parents and absence of others during Candlelight? Leaders can minimize concern by inviting all parents to the opening and closing of the Chrysalis event.

- *Candlelight in Chrysalis is for participants, not the parents.* Candlelight does not exist to convert parents or inspire them to attend an Emmaus event, as desirable as these responses would be. Event leaders face the temptation of tying the power of the Chrysalis ministry to the needs of people other than the participants (such as the team, kitchen crew, or parents) and to expand its model and policies to accommodate additional goals. Leaders need to avoid this temptation. The Chrysalis ministry cannot do all things and cannot bear the burden of accomplishing many aims without eventually compromising its only aim: spiritually forming young Christians and strengthening their associations with one another in the faith.

- *Non-Emmaus parents' participation in Candlelight "gives away" a special Emmaus moment to potential Emmaus participants.* Hopefully, parents will consider participating in Emmaus because of their youth's Chrysalis event experience and the changes that take place afterward. But their reaction to Candlelight out of context can negatively affect that possibility. Participation in that service will not enhance their own event experience.

- *Some young people need space from their parents and vice versa.* Though parents' appearance would surely be positive for some participants (and parents), the practice presents obstacles to grace for others.

Having outlined Candlelight's intent as internal to Emmaus Communities, note that *no policy can prohibit the presence of non-Emmaus parents at Candlelight.* Leaders cannot ban parents from a place or activity involving their sons and daughters. To do so would convey the false impression of secrecy, cult-like behavior, or inappropriate involvement with the young people. If parents know about Candlelight and insist upon participating, then sponsors deal with that fact as well as they can, accompanying them if necessary. If parents show up, they receive welcome. Members of the gathered Emmaus Community then do all they can to explain the context for Candlelight and to minimize these parents' sense of being out of place. Extraordinary circumstances may even warrant a parent's presence. The serving of Holy Communion obligates the gathered Community to welcome and receive everyone who wants to be near to God and to feast on the bread of life.

PSYCHOLOGICAL MANIPULATION

The Emmaus models for the live-in experiences of The Walk to Emmaus and Chrysalis provide time and space for the participants to take breaks, to rest, and to sleep. They are not lock-ins during which the participants are kept active late into the night. They are not religious marathons aimed at wearing the participants down physically, mentally, and emotionally. Event leaders who prolong the schedule late into the evening or who add structured activities that crowd out breaks and steal sleep time unwittingly participate in a form of psychological manipulation that has no place in the design or the proper manner of leading the experience.

Emmaus models its programs on faith in the power of God's presence in Christian Community, an appreciation for the value of extended time apart to focus on "the one thing necessary" and on respect for each person's dignity and freedom as a child of God. The intent of the time apart from the pressure of everyday activities is to provide space in which participants may hear and respond freely to the call of divine love.

SEXUAL HARASSMENT AND CHILD ABUSE LAWS

It is the Emmaus Community Board of Directors' responsibility to know the sexual harassment and child abuse laws of their state and to communicate them to the Chrysalis event team leaders, who then share that information with other team members. Event clergy team leaders remain highly vigilant to the possibility of abusive situations in the lives of young people and know the legal and pastoral steps to take if a case of abuse surfaces. While the event clergy team leaders may offer counsel to such persons and make helpful referrals, they must also abide by laws that require immediate reporting of instances of abuse to the authorities. Many states require a reporting of any information about possible child abuse and hold persons who have knowledge of abuse but do not report legally liable.

The local Chrysalis ministry, in cooperation with the sponsoring Emmaus Community Board of Directors, has a deep commitment to the safety and well-being of every person involved in a Chrysalis event. Leadership takes appropriate care to screen and supervise all volunteer team members and workers to ensure a safe environment for all participants at every Chrysalis event. The board uses the current practices and policies of The United Methodist Church annual conference in that area as the minimum standard for its work. The board will contact the United Methodist conference staff person in charge of youth ministry once a year to

- receive a clear statement of the current policies and practices, which then are conveyed to the appropriate persons supporting the local Chrysalis ministry, and

- confirm to The United Methodist conference staff person that the local Chrysalis ministry policies meet or exceed the standards of The United Methodist Church.

The Community Board can establish policies beyond the minimum standards of The United Methodist annual conference. The Board takes care not to place unnecessary burdens, fears, and obligations on the Chrysalis event volunteers and participants. The goals: be wise, prudent, fair, and positive; model Christian values in an atmosphere of love and trust; and joyfully assist young people in their spiritual lives.

SECTION 8— SUGGESTED SUPPLIES

EVENT SUPPLIES—AGAPE ROOM

✓	Item	Amount needed
____	Pens	6
____	Black permanent markers	3
____	Rubber bands	1 box
____	Stapler & staples	1 stapler & 1 box staples
____	Masking tape	1 roll
____	Scissors	1 pair
____	Clear adhesive tape	2 rolls
____	Paper clips	1 box
____	Stationery & notepaper	Several packages each
____	Envelopes, letter size	1 box
____	Correction fluid	1 bottle
____	Duct tape	1 roll
____	Screwdriver	1
____	Hanging file rack	2
____	Hanging file folders	2 boxes
____	Manila envelopes (info packets)	1 per participant and team member
____	Colored 3" x 5" index cards	1 package
____	Colored yarn	As desired
____	Sticky notes for labeling	2 packages
____	Reusable adhesive	As desired
____	Delivery baskets/boxes	As desired
____	*The Upper Room* daily devotional guide	1 per Closing packet (Call Customer Service at 1-800-972-0433)
____	Closing Packet contents	Group photo; Event Roster; Reference Lists; "Points to Remember" and "Things to Know;" Fourth Day Follow-up Meeting and Community Activities; "The Gift" flyer

EVENT SUPPLIES—REGISTRATION

✓	Item	Amount needed
———	Name tags, suitable for reuse at Gatherings	1 per participant & team member
———	Door tags and/or bed tags	1 per participant & team member

EVENT SUPPLIES—PRAYER CHAPEL

✓	Item	Amount needed
____	Large cross for table or floor	1
____	Event participant cross	1 per participant
____	Lanyards	1 per participant cross
____	Labels/tags	1 per participant cross
____	Candles (if the facility allows their use)	1 dozen
____	Bibles	2
____	Pens	6
____	List of team members	2
____	List of participants	2
____	Talk charts	3
____	CD or mp3 player	1
____	Recordings of music appropriate for Emmaus	6 CDs or other media
____	Songbook	6
____	Event *Worship Booklet*	6
———	Notepads for prayer requests	3
____	Altar materials	As needed
____	Hand crosses	6

EVENT SUPPLIES—CONFERENCE ROOM: GENERAL & ALTAR

✓	Item	Amount needed
____	Lectern	1
____	Microphone / sound system	1
____	Laptop, projector, screen	1
____	DVD of *Living Fully, Dying Well* Reflections	1
____	Easel	1
____	Bell	2
____	Basket for prayer requests and notepaper to write them on	1 basket, 3 notepads
____	Gallon-sized, zipper-lock plastic bags	50
____	3" x 5" index cards	2 packs
____	Staplers & staples	As desired
____	Hot glue gun & glue sticks	As desired
____	Reusable adhesive	As desired
____	Rubber bands	As desired
____	Notebook paper	As desired
____	Sticky notepads	As desired
____	Twine	As desired
____	Bible (Altar)	1
____	Christ Candle (Altar)	1
____	Small Table (Altar)	1
____	Matches / lighter (Altar)	1
____	Cross (Altar)	1
____	Butterfly tablecloth (Chrysalis)	1
____	Books for the book table	Purchase from The Upper Room or local Christian bookstore, or solicit donations. (See emmaus.upperroom.org for book suggestions.)
____	Communion elements and service ware	As determined by the event clergy team leader

EVENT SUPPLIES—CONFERENCE ROOM: TABLES & PARTICIPANTS

✓	Item	Amount needed
____	Small container to hold art supplies	1 per table
____	Box of colored markers	1 per table
____	Scissors	1 per table
____	Masking tape	1 roll per table
____	Pencils	6–8 per table
____	Box of crayons	1 per table
____	Transparent tape	1 roll per table
____	Small pencil sharpener	1 per table
____	Bottle of glue	1 small bottle per table
____	Hand-held hole puncher	1 per table
____	Bible	1 per table
____	Table name holder	1 per table
____	Tissues	1 per table
____	Snack dish or basket	1 per table
____	Poster board or poster paper	1–2 per talk per table, plus extra
____	Construction paper	3–4 per talk per table, plus extra
____	Trash bag	1 per table
____	Pens	1 per participant & team member
____	Notebook	1 per participant & team member
____	Songbook	1 per participant & team member
____	Folders	1 per participant & team member
____	Plastic cup	1 per participant & team member
____	Caterpillar, cocoon, and butterfly pins (Chrysalis)	1 each per participant & team member (made by Community)
____	Event *Worship Booklet*	1 per participant & team member (order from Upper Room)
____	Accountability Group Cards	1 per participant & team member (order from Upper Room)
____	Talk Reflection guides	1 per participant & team member for each talk
____	Talk Outline handouts	1 per participant & team member for each talk

EVENT SUPPLIES—CONFERENCE ROOM: HEALTH & BEAUTY AIDS

✓	Item	Amount needed
____	Combs	As desired
____	Bar Soap	As desired
____	Deodorant	As desired
____	Toothpaste	As desired
____	Toothbrush	As desired
____	Dental Floss	As desired
____	Mouthwash	As desired
____	Shampoo	As desired
____	Conditioner	As desired
____	Women's sanitary supplies	As desired
____	Razors	As desired
____	Shaving Cream	As desired

SECTION 9—SAMPLE LETTERS AND HANDOUTS

REGISTRAR'S LETTER ACKNOWLEDGING RECEIPT OF APPLICATION

The Registrar sends this letter to a participant candidate to acknowledge receipt of his or her application for an Emmaus Ministries event. Revise to fit the circumstances of the event and your Community.

Dear [Participant Candidate's First Name],

Your application and deposit for the [Community Name] Emmaus Community's [Emmaus Ministry] event have been received, and your application is on file by [Date of Receipt].

Invitations to attend a specific event are extended on a "first-come, first-served" basis, starting approximately [Number of weeks] weeks before the starting date of the event. Persons whose applications are received early ([Number of weeks] weeks or more ahead of the event) are highly likely to receive an invitation. If we received your application later than that, it is still likely you will receive an invitation; however, it is possible (especially if there was a waiting list from the previous event), that you will not receive an invitation until the following event.

When you receive your invitation, if the date does not work for you, you may decline the invitation; your application will be held, and you will be invited again for the next event.

Please contact me if you have any questions about Emmaus or the [Emmaus Ministry] event. We look forward to your participation!

Sincerely,

[Registrar's Name]
Registrar   Telephone: [Phone Number]
[Community Name] Emmaus Community   Email: [Email Address]

REGISTRAR'S ACCEPTANCE LETTER TO PARTICIPANT

The Registrar sends this letter to a participant when he or she is accepted to attend an Emmaus Ministries event. Revise to fit the circumstances of the event and your Community.

Dear [Participant's First Name],

We are glad that you have applied to attend [Event] # [Number], being held at [Event Location]. The [Community Name] Emmaus Community and the event team are already engaged in planning, preparation, and prayer for this event.

You have been accepted to participate in the event. It will begin on [Event Start Date] at [Event Start Time] and conclude on [Event End Date] at [Event End Time]. Please clear your schedule for the entire time of the event. It is imperative that nothing interrupt (phone calls, drop-in visits, outside concerns, etc.) this time. In case of emergency, your family will call your sponsor.

The event is casual, so bring comfortable clothes. Most of the time will be spent in the conference room, but there will also be time for an occasional walk outdoors, so plan accordingly. Bring your own toiletry items (soap, shampoo, towels) and bedding (sheets and blankets or sleeping bag and pillow); a mattress will be provided.

All meals and plenty of snacks will be provided during the event. You may want to consider bringing a small sum of money or a blank check to purchase Christian books or devotionals that will be available during the event.

Your sponsor will arrange to pick you up and bring you to the event. Similar arrangements will be made for the return home.

[*For Chrysalis*] Please remind your parent(s) that they are **invited and welcome** to attend the event's opening Send-Off and Parents' Meeting and the closing service.

Please contact me to confirm your participation or if you have any questions or concerns. The balance owed for the event is $[Balance Amount]; please bring that with you to the event (cash, or a check made out to the Community). We are looking forward to getting to know you and having you become a member of our Emmaus Community.

Sincerely,

[Registrar's Name]
Registrar
[Community Name] Emmaus Community

Telephone: [Phone Number]
Email: [Email Address]

REGISTRAR'S LETTER TO PARTICIPANT'S SPONSOR

The Registrar sends this letter to a sponsor when his or her participant has been accepted to attend an event. Revise to fit the circumstances of the event and your Community.

Dear Sponsor,

Your participant candidate, [Participant's Full Name], has been accepted for [Event] being held at [Event Location] on [Event Dates]. You may begin preparing now for [his/her] successful participation in this Emmaus event.

As a sponsor, the Community expects you to support the participant in the following ways:

- Prepare [him/her] for the event.

- [*For Chrysalis*] Reassure [his/her] parents about the event; invite [his/her] parents to the Send-Off and Closing and the Parents' Meeting (if there is one).

- Be a caretaker for [his/her] family; make yourself available for emergencies, fellowship, and spiritual support during the event.

- Ask [his/her] friends and family to show support by writing "personal agape" letters.

- Encourage and assist [him/her] in finding a spiritual support group after the event.

- Bring [him/her] to the first Community Gathering held after the event.

- Continue interest in and support of [his/her] spiritual welfare as a companion Christian.

Your specific responsibilities for the event are these:

- Arrange to bring your participant to the event location by [Event Start Time] and to take [him/her] back home after the event (after Closing).

- Stay with the participant through Send-Off; remain to participate in Sponsors' Hour. (If you cannot attend Sponsors' Hour, please have someone attend in your place).

- Share in the Candlelight at [Candlelight Location] on [Candlelight Date & Time].

- Share in the Closing at [Closing Location] on [Closing Date & Time].

Enclosed is an example of letter that you may use to request the "personal agape" letters. You will ask your participant's closest friends and family members (including [his/her] spouse, if applicable) to write personal letters to the participant; the letters are to be at the event location by [Agape Letter Date & Time]. These letters are *essential* to the event; it is extremely important that you follow through on this task. **We ask that the sponsor, friends, and family members provide** *only* **letters and** *not* **personal agape gifts.**

The event team appreciates your support. If you have any questions, please contact me.

Sincerely,

[Registrar's Name]
Registrar
[Community Name] Emmaus Community

Telephone: [Phone Number]
Email: [Email Address]

FOR CHRYSALIS: REGISTRAR'S LETTER TO PARTICIPANT'S PARENTS

The Registrar sends this letter to a Chrysalis event participant's parents to help them know what to expect. Revise to fit the circumstances of the event and your Community.

Dear Parent:

I am writing to share some information about the Chrysalis event your youth is attending at [Event Location]. To help you better understand what this event is about, I am enclosing a copy of the Chrysalis Statement of Purpose.

To explain briefly, chrysalis is the growth stage between a caterpillar and butterfly. While on the surface it may look as though nothing is happening, the delicate process inside transforms the caterpillar into a butterfly. For youth participating in Chrysalis, the chrysalis symbolizes our death to self so Christ can transform us into new beings. Through Chrysalis, youth are led to realize that Christ can transform them into something beautiful if they will open themselves to him and allow the transformation to occur.

The Chrysalis event is a powerful and moving experience in the sense that it puts youth in touch with the transforming power of God's love, which frees them to see and live life in a whole new way. The new way is God's way of love.

The young person you send to the Chrysalis event will probably not return home the same. Often youth will return having had a mountaintop experience and are filled with an abundance of joy and excitement—due to a spiritual encounter with Jesus Christ. It also comes from an intense time of fellowship with other people their age.

You can support your youth's Chrysalis experience through your openness to listen and share in his or her joy. You can also support your youth by encouraging him or her to continue growing spiritually through Bible study, prayer, daily devotions, and regular participation in a spiritual support group. We will encourage the young people to do these things, and modeling these practices in your own life will reinforce this message.

I'd like to add a word about the spiritual support group. The support group is made up of youth who have attended a Chrysalis event, as well as other interested youth. Each support group has an adult leader. The support group helps youth continue their spiritual growth. If you have no youth in your area, your son or daughter may choose to join an Emmaus group, which is the adult counterpart to Chrysalis.

Your youth's Chrysalis experience ends with a Closing service at [Closing Location], to which you are invited. Please arrive by [Parents' Closing Time] and meet in [Parents' Closing Location] so that all parents can proceed to the Closing service as a group. Your teen will appreciate your participation in this service, and I encourage you to attend.

Again, I appreciate your youth's participation. I encourage you to pray for and support your youth during and after this weekend. If I can be of any assistance to you and/or your youth, please do not hesitate to contact me. May God bless you.

Yours in Christ,

[Registrar's Name]
Chrysalis Registrar
[Community Name] Emmaus Community

Telephone: [Phone Number]
Email: [Email Address]

SPONSOR'S LETTER TO REQUEST AGAPE LETTERS FOR PARTICIPANT

The Sponsor sends this letter to a friend or family member of the participant to request a personal agape letter. Revise to fit the circumstances of the event and your Community.

Dear [Friend or Family Member's Name],

[Participant's Full Name] will be attending a [Name of Emmaus Ministry] spiritual renewal event at [Event Location] from [Event Start Date] to [Event End Date]. I am [his/her] sponsor for this event.

The [Community Name] Emmaus Community hosts the event and offers participants many gifts and surprises. At one point, the participants receive letters from family and close friends—a meaningful part of the experience.

Since you are someone special in [his/her] life, I am asking you to write a letter to [Participant's First Name]. Please keep it a complete surprise.

This is a special opportunity to tell [Participant's First Name] of your appreciation of [him/her] and what your relationship with [him/her] means to you. You may recall some personal event, even humorous, that the two of you shared. This may be your chance to record for [Participant's First Name] moments and events that you find difficult to say in person. This letter of love will be read *only* by [Participant's First Name].

After writing the letter and signing it,

- Put the letter in an envelope, and seal the envelope.
- PRINT "[Participant's Full Name]" on the front of the envelope.
- Do not write your name anywhere on the envelope.
- Put that envelope into a larger envelope, and mail or return it to

> [Sponsor's Name]
> [Street Address]
> [City, State, Zip]

- Mail your letter so I receive it by [Date: 1 week before the event].

Occasionally sponsors have to do a little detective work to get names and addresses of friends and family close to the participant. Please let me know the name and address of anyone you know that [Participant's First Name] would like to hear from.

Remember, this is supposed to be a surprise for [Participant's First Name]. But if [he/she] should ask, do not hide it, rather share that it will be a special part of the event. Thank you for making this event even more meaningful for [him/her].

Sincerely,

[Sponsor's Name]
[Sponsor's Phone Number]; 　　　　　　　　　　[Sponsor's Email Address]

EVENT SPIRITUAL DIRECTOR'S LETTER TO PARTICIPANT'S PASTOR

The Event Spiritual Director sends this letter to a participant's pastor at the conclusion of the event. Revise to fit the circumstances of the event and your Community.

Dear Pastor,

I am pleased to inform you, as a colleague and as one who has had temporary pastoral care for a member of your congregation, that [Participant's Full Name] attended [Ministry Event Name] on [Event Dates]. As you may know, [Ministry Event Name] is an Emmaus Ministry of The Upper Room and is held in our area at [Event Location].

Emmaus Ministries programs are designed to strengthen and renew the faith of its participants and, through them, to renew their families and congregations. An Emmaus event includes an experience of living in Christian community with daily prayer, Holy Communion, and discussion. The discussions take place around talks given by laypersons and clergy on the theme of God's grace and how that grace comes alive in the Christian community and the world. Emmaus also includes an ongoing support program after the event.

As the [Event]'s Spiritual Director, I encourage you to invite [Participant's First Name] to share what the [Event] meant to [him/her] and to discuss what [he/she] plans to do as a result. If a personal conversation is not possible, you can show your support and openness to [Participant's First Name]'s experience by sending [him/her] a card of congratulations for having attended. You could call or email to let [him/her] know you are aware of [his/her] participation. This will allow you to guide [him/her] into the most appropriate ways this experience can translate into servant leadership within your congregation and the larger body of Christ. The purpose of Emmaus Ministries is to strengthen the church. [Participant's First Name] may need your help to bridge the gap between the event experience and the post-event challenge of living out the faith.

Some people come away from their [Event] with great zeal and new priorities for their lives. Others come away feeling strengthened and confirmed in an already rich and lively faith. It seems that most everyone comes away having experienced God's love in Christ and desiring to pass it on in daily life. Many need their pastor to guide them in the best ways to grow this love.

If you have questions or concerns, please feel free to contact me or one of the other local clergy leaders in Emmaus: [Names & Phone Numbers of Emmaus Spiritual Directors].

Grace and peace,

[Event Spiritual Director's Name]
    [Event] Spiritual Director, [Community Name] Emmaus Community
    [Event] Spiritual Director's Phone Number

"POINTS TO REMEMBER" HANDOUT FOR THE PARTICIPANT'S PACKET

Revise to fit the circumstances of the event and your Community.

POINTS TO REMEMBER

Do not develop a holier-than-thou attitude. An Emmaus Ministries event is one of many instruments of spiritual renewal.

Do not bug people, especially clergypersons, to attend an Emmaus event. This can generate the impression that Emmaus is a requirement for authentic Christianity. It is not.

Do not compare an Emmaus event with a retreat. They are two different methods of renewal. They complement each other, but an Emmaus event is a once-in-a-lifetime experience.

Do not form a clique among yourselves. This is not Christlike and repulses those who have not attended an Emmaus Ministries event or who are not interested.

Do not act as though the Emmaus Community is a secret society. When people ask, tell them what Emmaus is and what your event meant to you.

Offer your services to your pastor. Together with him or her and other parishioners, you are the church in your community. You need the pastor, and the pastor needs your involvement in personal ministry. Refrain from criticizing your pastor.

When you wish to seek spiritual counsel or discuss a matter with your pastor, be courteous and ask when it would be convenient for him or her to see you. The pastor is your servant, yes, but the pastor also has many persons to serve. Don't think you deserve special attention because you have attended an Emmaus event.

Attend your weekly accountability group meeting and the Emmaus Community Gatherings. An Emmaus event does not pretend, nor is it able, to give a complete course in Christian formation. If you think you've arrived after your event, you're mistaken. You have just begun anew.

Act upon your Emmaus experience; your actions bear the greatest witness to the value of Emmaus. Upon returning from an Emmaus Ministries event, go to your pastor and ask how you can serve Christ's church more fully.

"THINGS TO KNOW" HANDOUT FOR THE PARTICIPANT'S PACKET

Revise to fit the circumstances of the event and your Community.

THINGS TO KNOW

Your Emmaus accountability group is the most important part of your Fourth Day. Be diligent in setting up one, and remain faithful to it. Don't be afraid to change groups if you don't feel comfortable in the group you join.

Emmaus Community Gatherings are held on: Date: _____

Time: _____ Place: _____

You can serve the Emmaus Community and express your support by working in the kitchen or on one of the support committees. Sign-up sheets for these committees are available at all Emmaus activities.

The Emmaus events' Candlelight and Closing services are for Emmaus Community members only. Guests are always welcome at the monthly Emmaus Community Gatherings. Children attend only the planned family activities.

[Your spouse is welcome to attend the post-event Follow-up Meeting this coming Tuesday. Following a Men's Walk to Emmaus event, the spouses who come on Tuesday night hear a talk by a board member and are given the opportunity to ask questions and discuss The Walk to Emmaus event in general.]

For future Emmaus events, if you are in the building when a talk is being presented, please remain in the dining area or the Prayer Chapel. No one is to linger in the hall outside the conference room and listen to the talk.

If you are working in the kitchen or are in the building for any reason, limit your contact with the event participants as much as possible. No one other than the kitchen crew joins the participants in the dining room. Spouses and sponsors do not serve in the dining room.

A Board of Directors governs the Emmaus Community. This group, which includes the Community Spiritual and Lay Directors, meets once a month to discuss problems and potential solutions, to formulate policy, to select future event team leaders, team members, and so forth. You may write to your board about anything that bothers or pleases you. If you want to bring a proposal, you ask to be added to the meeting agenda.

Emmaus is an instrument of Christian revitalization. Its purpose is to train leaders who will become solid leaders in their own church's ministries.

PRAYER PROMPTS FOR THE PRAYER CHAPEL

Revise to fit the circumstances of the event and your Community.

Begin your prayer vigil by asking God to clear your mind of all outside distractions.

Place your thoughts and spirit with the people and the event you are asking God to bless.

Be silent for a few seconds and begin to sense God's presence with you.

Pray as if you are talking to your best friend—you are!

Ask for the Spirit's blessing of the buildings, grounds, and all items used to bring those present to an awareness of God.

Pray for the [Lay Director or Team Leader], if not by name, by duty.

He or she must walk in God's Spirit to address any task that may arise.

Pray for the [Assistant Lay Directors, Assistant Team Leaders, or Coaches] that they may have the courage to sustain the purity of the event and not allow personalities to keep them from fulfilling their promises to God.

Pray that the [Spiritual Director] and Assistants be instruments of God's Spirit.

Pray that the speakers remember whom they represent, that they lay down self and glorify God.

Pray for the talks, for the messages given and received, that all may hear according to need.

Pray for the Musicians, that their music may bring God's message and soothe troubled souls.

Pray for the participants:

- the ones who cannot leave their thoughts behind

- the ones uneasy in the setting

- the ones who cannot sleep

- the ones looking for magic, not miracles

- the ones who are open and receiving

- for all the conditions known to God.

Pray for the [Agape, Facilities/Logistics, Kitchen, etc.] servants and all who minister in unrecognized ways.

Pray for the fun and fellowship that will warm hearts and keep the focus on God.

Pray for the Table Leaders that they do not tire. Pray for their renewed strength.

Pray for all the agape gifts, for the hands that made them and the blessing they bring.

Pray for the special times, such as chapel, agape feasts, Closing.

Pray for other Emmaus Communities.

Lastly, give all to our Lord and friend who sees and knows, asking for Jesus' blessing and presence with everyone connected to this event—not only those mentioned but also the families of the participants and leaders—and for the change for the church and Community.

Close by praising and thanking God for the opportunity given to intercede on behalf of God's children.

Amen.

SECTION 10— RESOURCES

EMMAUS PUBLICATIONS

The Board of Directors by Richard A. Gilmore. For members of the Emmaus board, this resource details the responsibilities of board members and board committees.

Coming Down from the Mountain: Returning to Your Congregation by Lawrence Martin. Encourages Emmaus participants to live out their obedience to Christ after returning from their Emmaus event.

The Early History of the Walk to Emmaus by Robert Wood. Written by the founding international director of The Walk to Emmaus, this book gives a personal firsthand account of the beginnings of The Upper Room's Walk to Emmaus ministry.

Fruit of the Spirit: The Way of Emmaus and Chrysalis by Cathi Eberly. Looks at each fruit of the Spirit (Galatians 5:22-23) and helps Emmaus leaders learn how to spread Spirit-filled attitudes and behaviors.

The Group Reunion by Stephen D. Bryant. Contains guidance on the spiritual purpose and practice of the group reunion (accountability group).

Leadership Development by Ideal Curtis. Learn how to delegate, prioritize, listen, serve humbly, and become more Christlike. Emmaus can revitalize your faith and help you lead as Christ's servant in your home, church, school, or workplace.

Music Directors and Song Leaders by Kate Dickinson and Gene Berrier. Guides music leaders in preparation for an Emmaus event, addressing such topics as why we sing, personal preparation, team formation, tips for effective song leading, how to plan music that flows with the event, and more.

One in the Spirit: The Emmaus/Chrysalis Relationship by David McKeown. Helps Emmaus Communities with Chrysalis ministries focus on their common mission, see their relationship as a partnership of ministry, treat each other with mutual respect, develop new leaders, realize the importance of mentoring, resolve conflicts, and strengthen and streamline the operations of the ministries.

The Role of Agape by Susan Jackson, with Cinda McCracken. Explains the various forms of agape and anonymous acts of servanthood that are vital to communicating unconditional love during each Emmaus event.

Spiritual Directors by Kay Gray. Addresses the role, qualifications, and responsibilities of Spiritual Directors before, during, and after the Emmaus event.

Spiritual Growth through Team Experience by Joanne Bultemeier. Covers qualities of a team member, spiritual benefits of team membership, what happens at team meetings, leadership development, and other aspects of being part of the Emmaus Conference Room team.

Sponsorship by Richard and Janine Gilmore. Explains the unique approach to recruitment for Emmaus: one person taking responsibility for another participant. Provides details of Emmaus sponsorship, beginning with why a person might choose to sponsor, whom to sponsor, the responsibilities of sponsors, and the commitment involved in sponsoring participants.

Sustaining the Spirit by William F. Gusey. Supplements event team manuals and describes the characteristics and conditions of team performance that are most conducive to creating and sustaining a spiritually dynamic atmosphere for an event.

Walking Side by Side: Devotions for Pilgrims by Joanne Bultemeier and Cherie Jones. Contains 45 meditations based on the talks given during an Emmaus event.

What Is Chrysalis? by Sharlyn DeHaven Gates. Introduces the ideas behind the Chrysalis ministry and describes what to expect during a life-changing Chrysalis event.

What Is Emmaus? by Stephen D. Bryant. Covers the purpose of Emmaus, what prospective participants need to know before attending, how Emmaus can benefit your church, why Emmaus holds separate events for men and women, and much more.

Your Questions Answered by Greg Engroff. Answers the most frequently asked questions about Emmaus.

Day Four: The Pilgrim's Continued Journey, revised edition by Robert Wood. A helpful resource that reminds participants of all that happened on the Emmaus event, expands on the talks, explains accountability groups and sponsorship, and offers ways participants can continue to grow in the image of Jesus Christ.

Fourth Day Forward: 60 Daily Meditations by various Emmaus event participants. Includes meditations on the Emmaus event's talk topics.

Taking Flight: 60 Daily Devos by various Chrysalis event participants. Includes meditations on the Chrysalis event's talk topics.

All of these resources are available online at bookstore.upperroom.org or by calling Customer Service at 800-972-0433.

FACE TO FACE RESOURCES

Selected Resources for Older Adults available on the Face to Face website Resources page http://facetoface.upperroom.org/resources.

OTHER RESOURCES

Celebration of Discipline: The Path to Spiritual Growth, by Richard J. Foster. Explores the central spiritual practices of the Christian faith; only by and through these practices can a person find the true path to spiritual growth.

SECTION 11—EVENT BACKGROUND ROLE DESCRIPTIONS

This section provides general descriptions of background or support roles that are common to most Emmaus Ministries events. For many of these roles, the responsibilities include carrying out policies as determined by the Community Board or ministry Steering Committee, so it is important that the Community leadership understands the definition of these roles and gives thought to their implementation for each of the supported Emmaus ministries. Detailed descriptions of these roles are included in each ministry's *Position-Specific Manual.*

The Upper Room Emmaus Ministries Office recommends that during preparations for an Emmaus event all coordinators and support servants meet together for mutual support. These meetings could include the following:

- Prayer for behind-the-scenes efforts, the Conference Room Team, and the participants;
- "Floating" accountability group sessions using the group card,
- Eucharistic celebration (ask the Community Spiritual Director to provide a clergyperson to celebrate Holy Communion),
- Explanation of anonymous servanthood and progressive servanthood,
- Discussions about true service (see chapter 9, "Discipline of Service," in *Celebration of Discipline* by Richard J. Foster).

Note: Because spiritual preparation for service is essential, behind-the-scenes support persons do not attend Conference Room Team meetings.

EVENT AGAPE COORDINATOR

Role

The Event Agape Coordinator works with the Agape Chair and/or Committee to plan the agape for an upcoming event. While the Agape Committee solicits and collects general agape from other Communities, the Event Agape Coordinator may work with the Agape Chair to inform the Community of particular needs of the upcoming Emmaus Ministries event. The coordinator then takes responsibility for collecting, organizing, and distributing agape throughout the duration of the event. This role may entail supervising and assigning other people various tasks during the event. By doing this, the coordinator trains and encourages others in servant leadership.

The Event Agape Coordinator guides other volunteers in service, being the hands of Christ, and ensuring that every participant experiences equal provision of agape love through the various gifts and symbols of agape. Although participants generally do not see the Event Agape Coordinator, this person's work creates the atmosphere of unconditional love and grace that inspires, heals, and transforms.

An Emmaus event requires three basic types of agape: general agape, table agape, and personal agape. A Chrysalis event also requires the Chrysalis symbols (caterpillar, cocoon, and butterfly). The Event Agape Coordinator enlists a helper for each type of agape to aid in securing, organizing, and distributing the agape. Enlisting the help of others in the Emmaus Community distributes the workload and helps pass on the model of Emmaus.

Responsibilities before the Event

The Event Agape Coordinator and all agape assistants attend the orientation session held before the first Conference Room Team meeting. In addition, assistants attend any meetings called by the Event Agape Coordinator. Such meetings help the servants learn and practice their individual roles for supporting the Emmaus event, pray for one another, and gain understanding about the boundaries of their service.

Other responsibilities of the Event Agape Coordinator include the following:

- Praying for the participants,
- Praying that God will inspire and empower the Emmaus Community to provide agape in the form of prayers, individual letters, snacks, and symbols that express the meaning and experience of Emmaus,
- Becoming familiar with The Upper Room's guidelines for agape (see "Guidelines for Agape" below),
- Securing supplies for the agape room (procuring a list from the Agape Chair or the person responsible for supplies); obtaining any missing supplies,
- Preparing the participants' packets.

Responsibilities during the Event

____ Set up an agape room to house all the agape just before the event.

____ Organize an area where people may drop off general agape and table agape before and during the event.

____ Prepare a box for the drop-off of personal letter agape if one is not provided; this will minimize traffic in the agape room.

____ Organize and distribute agape items at the appropriate times and to the appropriate places. (See the "Guidelines for Agape" below.)

____ Have banners, posters, or general agape letters ready and available for Conference Room Team members to share with participants throughout the event.

____ Collect, separate, and prepare the personal letters in bundles by the scheduled time.

____ Meet or check with other coordinators to see where responsibilities overlap.

____ Keep a record of all who help with agape during the event, and submit the names to the Agape Chair.

Guidelines for Agape

General Agape includes banners and letters for the group of participants from other Emmaus and Cursillo Communities all over the world or from accountability groups. These banners and letters declare God's love and indicate that others are praying for the participants.

Suggested Guidelines for General Agape

- Obtain general agape from the Agape Chair before the event begins.

- Open and sort general agape letters according to the specific phase of the event for which they are intended (keeping in mind the theme for each phase of the event).

- Make general agape letters available early in the event for the Conference Room Team members to share with the participants.

- Make banners available to decorate the conference room. Conference Room Team members will present and display these gifts for the participants gradually at fitting times during the event. Special banners may be stored and shared at other Emmaus events.

- Collect general agape at end of the event and return it to the Agape Chair.

Table Agape consists of the small gifts placed on the dining or conference room tables throughout the event. This agape may come from accountability groups, other members of the local Emmaus Community, individuals and other Emmaus Communities. Table agape expresses unconditional love; therefore, agape will have no names on it. Agape with names implies that the giver desires recognition or thanks.

The Agape Committee organizes and distributes table agape according to the day and time. It begins with a small amount given first and increases over the span of the event. Each participant receives the same agape. The Event Agape Coordinator routes all table agape.

Special gifts and notes for individual participants are inappropriate; these are returned to the sponsor. The Emmaus experience is designed to express God's love equally to everyone. For a Walk to Emmaus or Chrysalis event, any overabundance of agape for the dining room may be distributed as pillow agape.

Suggested Guidelines for Table Agape

- Inform the Community of your needs for table agape well before the Emmaus event.

- Collect table agape from the Emmaus Community and/or the Agape Chair.

- Ask those bringing agape to deliver items to the agape room by the start of the event and to provide enough pieces for everyone in the conference room.

- Remember that those serving behind the scenes do not receive agape. The support servants are present to serve and to make the Emmaus event run smoothly.

- Sort and label agape according to the time and place for distribution. Table agape begins at a specific time and day; distribute the agape while the participants are away from the tables.

- Distribute pillow agape on Friday evening for The Walk to Emmaus and Chrysalis; it is placed on each participant's pillow before the participants go to bed and while they are occupied elsewhere.

- Return all extra agape pieces to the agape room to give to those who donated them or follow an established board procedure.

- Clean up leftover agape items. If participants leave agape at the tables, put the items somewhere for retrieval.

Personal Agape letters, solicited by sponsors or designates, come to participants from family members, close friends, and occasionally members of the Emmaus Community. Each participant will receive no fewer than eight and no more than twelve letters at the appointed time in the schedule. This assures that each participant receives equal treatment and that participants will be able to read the letters in the time available.

The sponsor or sponsor designate has responsibility for making sure his or her participant has eight to twelve letters. Participants only receive individual agape letters near the end of the event at the time identified in the event schedule.

Personal agape does not include any type of personal items given only to one participant rather than to all. If gifts of more than twelve letters appear for an individual participant, return them to the sponsor before the Closing service. The sponsor will give them to his or her participant afterward.

Suggested Guidelines for Personal Agape
- Label boxes and sort letters in alphabetical order. For example, label one box for participants whose last name begins with letters A–G, another for names beginning with H–N, another with O–U, and another with W–Z. This allows helpers to sort letters as they come into the agape room.

- Collect personal agape from sponsors and designates.

- Provide a box for personal agape letters at the start of the event and before Candlelight.

- Ask Conference Room Team members to write a letter for any participants who have fewer than eight letters.

- Stack each individual's letters with family members' letters on top. Tie each stack with colorful ribbon or yarn. When more than twelve letters have been received for one participant, return the extra letters to the sponsor who gives them to the participant after Closing.

- Group the personal letters by table, using the table assignment list.
- Group each table's letters together in a sack or box. Place them in a room near the conference room. Make sure at least one assistant to the event lay team leader knows the location of the letters.
- Check all wastebaskets and other containers in the agape room to make certain that no letters have been accidentally discarded.
- Stuff the information packets with the necessary handouts. The board is responsible for their content and will provide these handouts (see the "Sample Letters and Handouts" section in this manual). If this is not done before the beginning of the Emmaus event, request copies from the Facilities Coordinator or whoever is responsible for supplies. Agape committee members may decorate the packet envelopes if desired.
- Break down the agape room and prepare to return items to storage before Closing and after distributing all packets and letters.

Caterpillar, Chrysalis, and Butterfly Pins represent the key metaphors of a Chrysalis event. These visible and tangible symbols of the themes are distributed as the Lay Director explains each theme.

Some Emmaus Communities face a challenge in finding or making these pins. The Agape Coordinator ensures that someone gets the pins made before the event, either by accountability groups, individuals who want to contribute to the event, or church members who want to be supportive. Craft shops stock the materials for making the pins.

EVENT FACILITIES COORDINATOR

Role

The Event Facilities Coordinator transports all supplies and equipment from storage to the event site and arranges for delivery to the right place. The amount of supplies and equipment requiring transport may vary depending on the facility used for the event.

A strong committee in this area offers a good place to start newer Community members in behind-the-scenes servanthood. Usually it takes several people to set up the facility in a fashion that satisfies the event's needs. Community leaders wisely employ veteran leaders to help orient and guide the new volunteers.

The Event Facility Coordinator and all assistants attend the orientation session held before the first Conference Room Team meeting. In addition, all assistants attend any meetings called by the Event Facilities Coordinator. Such meetings help the servants learn and practice their individual roles for the Emmaus event, prayerfully support one another, and gain understanding about the boundaries of their service.

Before setup begins, the Facilities Committee needs to understand the design of all areas within their responsibility. The Coordinator delegates a person to make a diagram of each room being used for the event, along with a list of equipment belonging to each room. Volunteers use this diagram at the end of the event to return the room to its original condition. This same person could also make a diagram of how to set up each room during the event, including placement of all Emmaus-related equipment. These diagrams will enable the efficient work of many support servants and create goodwill with those responsible for the host church/camp/retreat center.

The Facilities Coordinator and assistants set up the tables and chairs in the conference room, obtain the needed video equipment for showing the movie, make sure enough candles are available for Candlelight, move the large cross, and arrange for security for the event if necessary. At the close of the event, the Facilities Committee breaks down everything, returns the facility to its original condition, and returns all Emmaus Community equipment and supplies to storage.

Setup remains the same for all events unless the board approves a change. Consistency in setup from event to event makes it easier to use a variety of volunteers while maintaining quality assurance.

Responsibilities before the Event

____ Check with the Facilities Chair about inventory and make sure all supplies and equipment are available for the selected event dates—at least two weeks before the event.

____ Obtain any needed supplies or equipment.

____ Arrange for security personnel if needed.

____ Secure copies of the layout of each room (one diagram of the original setup of the room and a second diagram of setup for the Emmaus Ministries event).

Responsibilities during the Event

____ Begin setup early! The more time allowed, the less chance people will panic when something breaks or goes wrong. Committee members will also appreciate not being stressed at the last minute.

____ Transport all equipment and supplies to the event site.

____ Set up cots/mattresses (if the event includes overnight stays), tables, chairs, video equipment, etc. Know the exact number of people on the event (team and participants) so you can set up the correct number of chairs and tables in the chapel, conference room, and dining room.

____ Arrange various areas with the help of the assistants to the event lay team leader.

____ In the conference room, place chairs at the tables making sure there is an aisle for the speakers to enter. Be sure each participant can see each speaker, and that no table blocks anyone's line of vision. Set up the tables for the event team leaders and assistants in a row across the rear of the conference room. Set up the worship center at the front center of the conference room in front of the speaker's lectern. If using physical visual aids (such as posters, etc.), place an easel to one side of the speaker's lectern; put other equipment for visual aids in an easily accessible location. Test the audio and video equipment to be sure it works properly.

____ Place the large cross in the designated location (chapel/sanctuary) for Sponsors' Hour. If there is no Sponsors' Hour or at the conclusion of Sponsors' Hour, place the large cross in the Prayer Chapel.

____ In the chapel or sanctuary that serves as the worship setting for the event, place lecterns where needed for any speaking or music that will take place.

____ Allow older volunteers to help with lighter work duties in order to avoid injury or strain.

____ Make sure all areas are ready for the event. Do not leave set-up work for the Conference Room Team.

____ If the event used cots/mattresses, arrive early on the last morning to remove the mattresses and/or cots and return them to storage.

____ Once the event has concluded, take down tables, chairs, etc.

____ Clean all rooms and return them to their original condition. (Use diagrams to check each room.)

____ Inventory all supplies and equipment, and make a list of needed supplies.

____ Return inventory and supply list to the Facilities Chair.

____ Return all equipment and unused supplies to storage. This minimizes lost and missing items. A Supplies Chair may be in charge of the storage location and will maintain much of the Community inventory.

____ Remember, use as many Emmaus Community members as is practical in this support role, which provides servant opportunities and a feeling of ownership within the Community.

____ Provide a list of names of all those participating on this support committee to the Facilities Chair.

Handling Luggage

For a live-in event, the Event Facilities Coordinator may appoint a committee to handle the luggage. Basically, this responsibility consists of moving the participants' and Conference Room Team's luggage from the Send-Off location to their respective sleeping quarters and returning luggage to the Closing location at the end of the event. The Registrar will supply all the names and sleeping assignments for the participants and team members. With this information, the luggage handlers can proceed with the suggested tagging instructions listed below.

The following method has worked for many Communities:

- Secure enough volunteers to handle luggage efficiently when people arrive and when they leave.

- Have enough covered vehicles to move the luggage to the sleeping quarters if Send-Off is in a separate location from the sleeping quarters.

- Buy wire tags (4 ¼"x 2 ⅛"—10 point, 1000 per box) for luggage that are easily attached. Consider a piece of luggage to be any separate piece being transported (handbag, sleeping bag, pillow, blanket, etc.). Each tag will show the person's name and preassigned sleeping quarters. Assume four (4) tags per person, and insert the four tags into a 3" by 5" manila envelope along with the person's name tag. Write the person's name and sleeping quarters on the outside of the envelope.

- Hand out the wire tags with each name tag along with sleeping quarters assignment at Send-Off.

At the end of the event, the assistants to the event lay team leader will instruct participants and team members to pack their luggage, carefully tagging each piece. Someone from the luggage team will check the sleeping quarters to be sure all pieces are picked up. If that person finds any stray pieces, he or she takes them to Closing to be claimed. After Closing, double-check to see if any luggage remains. If so, a member of the luggage team may have to make a home delivery or take the luggage to the next Gathering.

EVENT KITCHEN COORDINATOR

Role

The Event Kitchen Coordinator recruits volunteers for the kitchen through a sign-up sheet at Gatherings, from accountability groups, or from the volunteer sign-up sheets new Community members receive at the end of their Emmaus events. Emmaus Community members may volunteer to work in the kitchen for all or part of an event. The Kitchen Chair fields all questions and communicates information.

The Event Kitchen Coordinator may purchase the food (if requested by the Kitchen Chair) and assumes responsibility for preparing meals and/or refreshments for the team and participants throughout the Emmaus event. The board decides if the team requires an additional meal prior to the event.

The kitchen provides snack agape for the conference room. The event leadership may decide to provide snacks for the participants and Community during the event check-in. If needed, select a Snack Assistant to solicit and organize the snacks for the event.

The Snack Assistant and helpers keep the snack table supplied throughout the event. The kitchen volunteers, under the direction of the Event Kitchen Coordinator, help prepare and serve the meals and aid with cleanup after meals. The facility may determine the number of kitchen servants needed. All kitchen volunteers may assist in praying for special needs throughout the event when kitchen responsibilities do not fill their time.

Models for Kitchen Staff

The kitchen servants are part of the behind-the-scenes support servants. They witness through their humble service and joy in giving without need for recognition. Introductions at mealtimes are not appropriate. Kitchen servants remain anonymous in their servanthood and invisible except when serving meals. They honor the cloistered environment of the conference room and refrain from interaction with the participants and team members as much as possible. Below are different ways to organize kitchen staff:

1. **Revolving:** The Event Kitchen Coordinator, with the help of the Kitchen Chair, enlists persons to serve over the course of two or three months. The Kitchen Coordinator organizes the kitchen and coordinates a revolving team of kitchen staff who have signed up to help prepare and serve meals at specific times during the Emmaus event. Though volunteers come and go, the Kitchen Coordinator remains on-site for the entire event. Recruit kitchen helpers from the Emmaus Community at Gatherings and at other times by asking people to sign up on a chart to work specific mealtimes. The advantages of this approach are these: not having to house and care for an entire kitchen crew, giving more Community members the opportunity to serve, needing fewer persons to make commitments for the entire event, and allowing the witness of so many Community members who take time to serve the participants.

2. **Live-in:** For a live-in Emmaus event (Walk to Emmaus, Chrysalis, or a live-in Journey to the Table event), remote event sites sometimes require kitchen servants who remain at the site throughout the event. These servants occupy separate sleeping quarters, away from the conference room participants. Live-in kitchen staff may care for other behind-the-scenes functions, such as decorating the dining room for a special meal, providing mealtime entertainment, or participating in the prayer room for the speakers and participants.

3. **Facilities that serve the meals:** Some events will have no kitchen servants because the retreat center's personnel prepare all the refreshments and meals. The food is offered either buffet style or served by other Emmaus Community members who come to the event site to decorate, serve, and clean the dining room. Servers may come from other behind-the-scenes support staff. If more than one group at a time is using the facility, set apart a section of the dining room for the conference room group.

Whichever model the event employs, kitchen volunteers provide the prayer and logistical support needed for the participants. This is their act of agape for the participants.

The Event Kitchen Coordinator and all assistants attend the orientation session held before the first Conference Room Team meeting. All support assistants attend any meetings called by the Event Kitchen Coordinator.

Other responsibilities of the Kitchen Coordinator include the following:

• Plan ahead and enlist others to assist with recruiting kitchen volunteers and preparing for the Emmaus event.

- Use a variety of Emmaus Community members in the kitchen as helpers, cooks, and servers: male and female; youth and adults; laity and clergy. *Sponsors and family members of event participants may work in the kitchen but do not serve in the dining room, as they remain unseen.*

- Remind the staff to be friendly, courteous, and cheerful. Always smile. Aloof, grumpy, or reluctant volunteers can undermine the atmosphere of the Emmaus experience.

- Remind volunteers of their commitment to *serve*, to offer more food or drink—not to converse with team members or participants.

- Ask the staff to remove their name tags when serving.

- Adjust the kitchen schedule to conform to the conference room schedule. Some facilities that prepare the food specify mealtimes, and the conference room honors these times. The assistants to the event lay team leader will coordinate any time changes with the Event Kitchen Coordinator.

- Minimize background noise when the kitchen and dining room are within hearing distance of the conference room or chapel.

- Do not introduce or excessively acknowledge the kitchen staff or servers. This diminishes the value of the kitchen servants' witness as anonymous servants, places an expectation on the participants to respond, uses valuable time, and interrupts the cloistered environment of the Emmaus event.

- Check with the Kitchen Chair to determine if the Emmaus event has established a standard menu. An established menu saves the Event Kitchen Coordinator time and trouble and frees the kitchen servants from the need to equal or outdo past Emmaus events. It also makes the cost predictable and sets a standard for quality. Each Emmaus Community develops a standard menu that is economical, nutritionally balanced, generous, and appealing. If necessary, consult a dietitian, nurse, or nutritionist for help. Obtain information about participants' special dietary needs from the Registrar.

- Alert the person purchasing food of any special food needs.

- Ensure that ice water is always available at the snack table, at meals, and in the conference room. Provide drinking cups for each participant at the conference room tables.

- Kitchen staff and other behind-the-scenes personnel eat in a separate space after all are served or may wait until the conference room group has been dismissed from the dining room. If this is not possible, they eat in shifts at a separate table, allowing half the group to be available to serve at all times.

- Provide ample food for the participants and team. If a shortage occurs, the support servants supplement the food.

- Provide Communion elements for each Communion service, if the Spiritual Director does not make this provision. If Communion is served at a team commissioning service prior to the event, plan for that, as well as for times during the event that the behind-the-scenes personnel take Communion.

Responsibilities Three Months before the Event

____ Check with the Kitchen Chair for an inventory list and learn how the Kitchen Chair will support your responsibilities.

____ Enlist an assistant for the kitchen's organizational needs.

____ Make a chart that lists all refreshments and meals, including times, during the Emmaus event.

____ Take the chart to Gatherings to enlist volunteers for the kitchen.

____ Invite accountability groups to serve together or assist in preparing a meal together.

____ Plan the meals according to the established menu. (Check with the Kitchen Chair for this menu.)

____ Request a variety of snack items from the Community by publicizing at Gatherings.

Responsibilities Two Weeks before the Event

____ Contact the treasurer to make arrangements for paying for the food and supplies.

____ Arrange for the purchase and delivery of food items if requested to do so by the Kitchen Chair.

____ Check with the Kitchen Chair to see if the team will require an extra meal before check-in for the event. If so, determine how many will be eating and who will prepare the meal.

____ Post a schedule of talks and prayer times in the kitchen area.

____ Develop at the meeting of the behind-the-scenes coordinators a schedule that lists all essential times and activities.

Responsibilities at the Start of the Event

____ Be sure food and supplies have been collected and delivered to the proper location.

____ Follow up on arrangements if the team will eat before check-in, and have enough people to help prepare and serve the meal.

____ Prepare the snacks for check-in and Send-Off with the help of the Snack Assistant.

____ Post the event schedule to encourage the kitchen staff to be in an attitude of prayer for the conference room group.

____ Double-check special dietary requirements with the Registrar or the assistants to the event lay team leader.

Responsibilities during the Event

____ Stay on schedule with the refreshments and meals, following the event schedule.

____ Maintain a servant attitude and be willing to adjust the kitchen schedule to accommodate the conference room activities when necessary.

____ Prepare the tables with table agape before each meal at the direction of the Agape Coordinator, observing the agape guidelines.

____ Remind volunteers that the Emmaus model calls for servants to remain as invisible as possible as they go about their tasks.

____ Maintain a good spirit and camaraderie among the kitchen servants.

____ Supervise kitchen volunteers and servers during the event.

____ Keep a list of names of those who have helped, and submit it to the board Kitchen Chair for future reference.

____ Be an encourager and teach others the joy of faithful service.

____ Be a mediator when necessary.

Responsibilities after Meal Service Is Over

____ Inventory, label, and pack up any supplies and nonperishable items for use at the next event.

____ (*Optional*) Distribute perishable foods to local soup kitchens. Some snacks may be used at a subsequent Gathering or Fourth Day Follow-up Meeting.

____ Clean the kitchen completely, and remove all trash. As guests in the facility, plan to leave it cleaner than when you arrived.

EVENT MUSIC / ENTERTAINMENT COORDINATOR

Role

The Event Music/Entertainment Coordinator arranges for any music needed outside the conference room, especially any after-meal entertainment. The Music Coordinator selects fitting after-meal entertainment that lasts between fifteen to twenty minutes.

The Event Music/Entertainment Coordinator and all assistants attend the orientation session held before the first Conference Room Team meeting. All support assistants attend any meetings called by the Event Music/Entertainment Coordinator. These meetings help the servants learn and practice their individual roles for supporting the Emmaus event, prayerfully support one another; and gain understanding about the boundaries of their service.

Other duties of the Music/Entertainment Coordinator include these:

- Enlist musicians besides those serving in the conference room. These musicians will assist with any music at the event Send-Off. In addition, they provide the music at the Emmaus Community Communion service before Candlelight. During Candlelight they lead the Community in singing "Jesus, Jesus." When the Community singing ends, these musicians do not lead the conference room group in singing to the Community.

- Arrange for any required after-meal entertainment. The entertainment should be light, humorous, and no longer than fifteen to twenty minutes. Do not enlist participants' family members for the entertainment. Enlist different people for the entertainment at each event so that the number of experienced persons available for each event increases; this is part of leadership development.

EVENT PRAYER CHAPEL COORDINATOR

Role

The Prayer Chapel Coordinator has the responsibility for prayer support for the entire Emmaus event. Prayer is a vital part of our growth as Christians, and it is an essential part of the training and preparation for an Emmaus Ministries event. Continuous prayer enhances the spiritual environment for the Emmaus experience.

Organized prayer takes place through the Prayer Chapel and the event's prayer vigil. The Prayer Chapel Coordinator solicits prayer support for the speakers, participants, and team; sets up a room for use as a Prayer Chapel during the event; leads the support servants in meditation and prayer times when convenient and appropriate, or enlists the assistance of a nonconference room clergyperson to provide this support. The Prayer Chapel Coordinator may choose to appoint one or two assistants to participate with him or her in the Prayer Chapel during the event to pray for the speakers or the participants and any prayer requests received during the event.

During the event, Community members may go to the Prayer Chapel before a talk and pray briefly with the speaker in preparation for a talk. They remain in prayer during the talk to support the speaker—this is prayer agape. Prayer Chapel agape is a powerful and dynamic way for members of the Emmaus Community to support the event by offering their prayers and presence on behalf of the speakers, the Conference Room Team, and the participants. The Prayer Chapel Coordinator also participates in this prayer time with each speaker.

The Prayer Chapel Coordinator designates a room at the Emmaus site for use as a Prayer Chapel. Throughout the event, people come unnoticed to the Prayer Chapel to pray for the speakers; to participate in the event's prayer vigil; and to pray for the participants, the Conference Room Team, and everyone serving behind the scenes. Those who pray remain unnoticed throughout the event. *The Prayer Chapel is not the same space as the chapel or sanctuary where participants worship during the event.* The designated Prayer Chapel is away from the participants' flow of traffic.

The Event Prayer Chapel Coordinator and all assistants attend the orientation session held before the first Conference Room Team meeting. All support assistants attend any meetings called by the Event Prayer Chapel Coordinator. These meetings help the servants learn and practice their individual roles for supporting the Emmaus event, prayerfully support one another, and gain understanding about the boundaries of their service.

The Prayer Chapel Coordinator sets up and maintains the Prayer Chapel throughout the event. In the Prayer Chapel, set up an area with a large cross (with participants' neck crosses hung on it), a candle, a Bible, two hand crosses for speakers, and anything else that will make the room conducive to prayer. Devotional material and aids to prayer can help persons who are unaccustomed to praying for extended periods (see "Prayer Prompts for the Prayer Chapel" in the Sample Letters and Handouts section in this manual). If using background music, play it at a low volume; some persons have difficulty concentrating on prayer with any kind of noise. Display the participants' neck crosses in the Prayer Chapel throughout the event to provide a prayer focus on behalf of the participants. Also provide lists of participants' and Conference Room Team members' names.

Responsibilities before the Event

_____ Enlist as many people from the Emmaus Community as possible to pray for the team members and participants throughout the event.

_____ Encourage those who pray to come to the Prayer Chapel at the event site and pray for particular speakers at the specified time. If they cannot come to the event site, ask them to pray wherever they are during the time of the talk.

_____ Prepare charts with the names of the talks, the speakers, and the date and times after the selection of the Conference Room Team.

_____ Ask speakers to name persons from whom they would like support and to solicit the attendance of Emmaus Community members.

_____ Send those persons a card or letter requesting their prayers and presence for the speaker at the designated time.

_____ Provide Prayer Chapel agape for the speakers and participants through the behind-the-scenes support servants if holding the event in more remote areas.

_____ Make arrangements with a Fourth Day clergyperson to provide Communion one time during the event for the support servants, if desired.

Responsibilities before Registration Check-in

_____ Set up and maintain the Prayer Chapel throughout the Emmaus event as described earlier in this section.

_____ Arrange the cross, Bible, two hand crosses for speakers, candle, etc.

_____ Designate, with the help of an assistant to the event lay team leader, a separate room for the table chapel visits.

_____ Place charts with speakers' names and talk times in the agape room, the Prayer Chapel, and other appropriate places.

Responsibilities during the Event

____ See that the large cross with the participants' neck crosses gets moved to the Prayer Chapel after Sponsors' Hour.

____ Arrange a convenient time to pray with other support servants.

____ Keep a record of any assistants who have helped you in the Prayer Chapel.

____ Put the hand cross in each speaker's hand prior to his/her talk.

____ Be present for prayer with each speaker before, during, and after the talk.

____ Return the hand cross to its place on the table.

____ Do not reveal any names associated with prayer requests that come to the Prayer Chapel. Display the requests and destroy them after the event.

____ Be available to assist in other behind-the-scenes areas when needed and make sure someone is praying in the Prayer Chapel.

____ Place a hand cross (or two hand crosses) on the lectern at Closing.

____ Return other hand crosses and items used to create the Prayer Chapel (with the exception of your own personal items) to the person responsible for supplies.

____ Provide the Prayer Chair with a list of assistants who helped.

Prayer Vigil

The local Emmaus Community provides prayer support for the event, participants, and team by organizing and staffing a prayer vigil. With the Prayer Chapel Coordinator's encouragement, Community members sign up on a chart for the event time slots during which they will pray. Accountability groups can participate by taking a block of time.

Members of the local Emmaus Community staff the entire prayer vigil. The Community may ask other Emmaus Communities around the world to hold a second prayer vigil. This effort supplements but never replaces the local Community prayer vigil. This prayer supplement ensures that prayer surrounds the event for its duration. The vigil represents prayer on the part of those who sign up, not just the appearance of prayer. Prayer vigil servants may, if they desire, come to the event site to pray in the Prayer Chapel at their chosen times or may pray wherever they are during their assigned time slot.

For live-in events (such as Walk to Emmaus, Chrysalis, etc.), the prayer vigil covers the entire event period, including times when the participants and team are sleeping. For these events, staff lock the event site facilities from late night to early morning; therefore, the Prayer Chapel is not accessible to prayer vigil servants at those times.

Event leaders share the prayer vigil chart with the event participants at some point during the event. The prayer vigil chart gives the participants a tangible sign of the loving support of many on their behalf, especially when they see the names of persons who have pledged to interrupt their schedules (including getting up at various hours of the night) to pray for them.

_____ Make a poster showing thirty-minute time slots for the Emmaus Ministries event (from the start through the end of Closing for a live-in event or covering each of the sessions for a non-live-in event).

_____ Bring the poster to Emmaus Gatherings preceding the event so Community members can choose times and sign their names in the chosen time slots.

_____ Recruit other Community members to fill any remaining time.

_____ Obtain a complete roster of your Emmaus Community to use when calling to ask for volunteers. Call on new members from recent events as well as homebound Community members.

_____ Involve Fourth Day Community members in outlying areas of the local Community. These groups may agree to accept time blocks to be filled by members of their local group. (Be sure to get specific names for each person filling a slot.)

_____ Recruit several people to do the calling, especially if you have a large number of empty time slots. Fill the remaining slots at Send-Off or ask persons who come to the Prayer Chapel to volunteer their time in prayer.

_____ Bring the poster with the prayer vigil time slots completely filled and give it to the event clergy team leader [Spiritual Director] at the start of the event.

EVENT REGISTRAR

Role

The Event Registrar, who may or may not be a member of the board or ministry Steering Committee, administers policies set by the Community Board or ministry Steering Committee. These policies include, but are not limited to, the upper limit on the number of event participants, the upper limit on the number of event participants from any one church, the cutoff date for receipt of event applications, the number of applications needed to justify holding the event (each event requires at least twenty confirmed participants two weeks before the dates of the event), the receipt of event fees, and the transfer of monies received to the treasurer.

In most of these activities, the Registrar serves as host to the participants who have been invited as guests to this event. All the activities of the Event Registrar are designed to make the participants feel as comfortable and as welcome as possible.

The Event Registrar assembles a proficient committee to assist with the responsibilities, including assisting with registration check-in at the start of the event. Effective committees are part of The Upper Room Emmaus model, and they offer one avenue of developing leaders for Emmaus and the church.

The Event Registrar and all assistants attend the orientation session held before the first Conference Room Team meeting. All support assistants attend any meetings called by the Event Registrar. These meetings help the servants learn and practice their individual roles for supporting the Emmaus event, prayerfully support one another, and gain understanding about the boundaries of their service.

Responsibilities before the Event

____ Receive applications and deposits.

____ Transfer funds to the treasurer.

____ Review applications/registrations for completeness in relation to the policies set by the board—for example, clergy signature by the participant's pastor, appropriate church affiliation, etc.

____ Work with the candidate or the sponsor to resolve questions and complete any missing information.

____ Present unusual questions not covered by board policy to the Registrar Chair for future board action. (The role of the Event Registrar is to follow policy; the board establishes policy.)

____ Send notifications of receipt of application and acceptance to each participant and sponsor (see the "Sample Letters and Handouts" section in this manual).

____ Give each sponsor a copy of instructions related to effective sponsorship for the event being held at this particular time and place.

____ Send a list of participants' names to the event lay team leader and to the communications team.

____ Prepare a list of special medical needs and dietary requirements. Send the list of medical needs to the event lay team leader and the list of dietary needs to the Event Kitchen Coordinator.

____ Submit scholarship requests to the individual assigned this task by the board.

____ Prepare a waiting list for the next event if necessary, and notify sponsors of those who are on the list.

Responsibilities during the Event

____ Greet the new participants at event check-in, and collect the balance due for registration fees. Have participants confirm the spellings of their names, their addresses, etc., and make necessary corrections. Employ the help of committee members in this process.

____ Transfer funds received to the treasurer.

____ Prepare a complete list of the new participants and submit it to the Prayer Chapel Coordinator and, if applicable, the individual responsible for Sponsors' Hour.

____ After the event has started, prepare a complete list of the new participants and the Conference Room Team with names, addresses, telephone numbers, and email addresses. Give this list to the individual responsible for making copies for the participants' packets.

Responsibilities after the Event

____ Prepare an audit of all funds handled for the specific event.

____ Submit a copy of the audit to the treasurer.

____ Send a corrected list of participants' names with complete contact information to the communications team.

____ Email the corrected list of participants' names and contact information (in Word, Rich Text, or Excel format) to The Upper Room Emmaus Ministries Office: emmaus@upper-room.org.

____ Supply a list of the names of all who worked as registration support assistants to the Registrar Chair or to the person who records information related to progressive servanthood.

EVENT SPONSORS' HOUR COORDINATOR

Role

The Community hosts a Send-Off and a Sponsors' Hour for events that require each participant to have a sponsor. These are typically live-in events; for these events, the sponsors bring their participants to the event site and remain with them until all team members and participants are sent off by the gathered Community to the conference room to begin the event (Send-Off). The sponsors then meet for a time of prayer and worship before returning home (Sponsors' Hour).

The Event Sponsors' Hour Coordinator ensures that the Community conducts Sponsors' Hour according to board guidelines. The Coordinator will need several individuals to assist with tasks.

The Event Sponsors' Hour Coordinator and all assistants attend the orientation session held before the first Conference Room Team meeting. All support assistants attend any meetings called by the Event Sponsors' Hour Coordinator. These meetings help the servants learn and practice their individual roles for supporting the Emmaus event, prayerfully support one another, and gain understanding about the boundaries of their service.

Responsibilities before the Event

____ Ascertain the number of participants by checking with the Event Registrar. Obtain the proper number of neck crosses and lanyards, plus a few extras in case of last-minute registrations.

____ Find out which room in the facility will be used for Sponsors' Hour.

Responsibilities before Send-Off

____ Arrange to have the large cross placed in the room where Sponsors' Hour will be held.

____ Place the neck crosses on the lanyards, and distribute them at the front of the room for easy access by the sponsors.

____ Have one copy per person if using an order of worship or other handout.

The leader keeps Sponsors' Hour brief; *hour* is simply a term used to describe this time. Sponsors will enter the chapel in an attitude of prayer. The leader opens the service with prayer. As the leader calls each participant's name, the sponsor places the participant's cross on the large cross. After delivering the participant's cross, the sponsor may choose to kneel and pray for the participant. If a sponsor cannot attend Sponsors' Hour, he or she finds a designate. If no one present accepts the participant's cross, assign a Community member to deliver the neck cross. The leader encourages Fourth Day Community members to attend Sponsors' Hour in case they are needed for this task.

After delivering all the crosses, those in attendance may sing a song and close the ceremony with prayer. After the service, the crosses will be moved to the Prayer Chapel and will remain there until the Closing service. In the Prayer Chapel, Community members pray for the participants by name throughout the event.

EVENT CANDLELIGHT SERVICE COORDINATOR

Role

The Event Candlelight Service Coordinator prepares everything for the Community gathering/ prayer/Communion service and takes responsibility for the Candlelight service details. The Coordinator will require assistance.

The Event Candlelight Service Coordinator and all assistants attend the orientation session held before the first Conference Room Team meeting. All support assistants attend any meetings called by the Candlelight Service Coordinator. These meetings help the servants learn and practice their individual roles for supporting the Emmaus event, prayerfully support one another, and gain understanding about the boundaries of their service.

Responsibilities

The Candlelight Service Coordinator will arrange for the many helpers needed for this service. Helpers include those who will distribute and collect bulletins and songbooks, those who will collect and tally the offering, musicians for the service (*not* the conference room musicians), the clergyperson who will lead the Communion service, possibly a Fourth Day speaker, and those who will serve the Communion elements.

The Coordinator appoints a suitable number of people to obtain supplies and bring them to the proper room. These individuals will collect the supplies and return them to the Candlelight Service Coordinator at the close of the service.

The Coordinator also asks several persons to assist with the distribution, lighting, and collecting of candles. They return the candles to the Candlelight Service Coordinator and inform the Coordinator of their status. The Coordinator transmits this information to the Sponsors' Hour/Candlelight Service chairpersons.

Specifics of Candlelight vary significantly for the different Emmaus Ministries events. In particular, the Candlelight service for a Face to Face event takes place during the day, and the event participants remain seated while the Community members process into the room and surround them. Refer to the individual ministries' *Position-Specific Resources Manual* and *Directors' Manual* for more details.

Importance of Candlelight

The Community assembles as they would for a Gathering. This reinforcement of the Fourth Day Community is a key activity for the event. Anyone who has attended a Fourth Day event (Emmaus or other) may attend Candlelight. Sponsors attend Candlelight as part of good sponsorship. Some individuals may travel across the country to attend the event. One advantage of holding the event at a local church is that it allows for maximum Community involvement, and a sanctuary is available for Candlelight.

The assembled Community prays for each participant by name and for the team as a whole. The service is scheduled to accommodate all the activities of the event.

EVENT SUPPLY / LITERATURE COORDINATOR

Role

The Supply/Literature Coordinator has a thorough knowledge of the materials required for an Emmaus Ministries event. The Coordinator works with the Supply/Literature Chair to ensure the proper amount of supplies and literature for the event. While one person can usually handle this job for the event, include at least one additional person to train for future events.

The Event Supply/Literature Coordinator and all assistants attend the orientation session held before the first Conference Room Team meeting. All support assistants attend any meetings called by the Event Supply/Literature Coordinator. These meetings help the servants learn and practice their individual roles for supporting the Emmaus event, prayerfully support one another, and gain understanding about the boundaries of their service.

Responsibilities

The Supply/Literature Coordinator maintains an accurate inventory of the supplies needed for the event to avoid shortages or overages. These may cause undue panic or pressure on the Community's expense budget. Much of the event's success depends on having the proper supplies, which makes this position critical.

The Supply/Literature Coordinator in most Communities not only orders the conference room supplies (notepads, pens, index cards, folders, etc.) but also the participants' lanyards and crosses, the speaker's hand crosses, worshipbooks, accountability group cards, and any other items. (Some of these items are available through The Upper Room.) Several people can share these responsibilities if desired, but many Communities have experienced better control if one person oversees supplies.

The person in charge of supplies/literature stands ready to run errands when unexpected needs arise during an event.

The Coordinator develops a complete list of all Community needs in a supply/literature manual so supplies and literature will be accurately tracked. Communities often have a person in training for this position at all times; it can be the most demanding of the behind-the-scenes jobs. Find suggested checklists in the "Suggested Supplies" section of this manual.

For the live-in events, most Emmaus Communities provide a "personal needs" supply basket, containing such items as over-the-counter medicines, toothpaste, toothbrushes, shampoo, adhesive strips, earplugs, and so forth. The Supply/Literature Coordinator usually has the responsibility of keeping this basket stocked.

EVENT TRANSPORTATION / HOUSING COORDINATOR

Role

The Transportation/Housing Coordinator and all assistants attend the orientation session held before the first Conference Room Team meeting. All support assistants, whether at the event location or involved in transportation, attend any meetings called by the Transportation/Housing Coordinator. These meetings help the servants learn and practice their individual roles for supporting the Emmaus Ministries event, prayerfully support one another, and gain understanding about the boundaries of their service.

When it is necessary to transport the team and participants from one site to another, one large church bus may serve the needs of the Community. Many Communities use vans. These usually don't require a special driver's license as do the large buses but meet the state's requirements in this matter. Be prepared with alternate transportation in the event of mechanical problems.

If transportation is required, use one driver per vehicle for the entire event to alleviate risk and confusion. The Emmaus Community carries adequate insurance even if the church that owns the vehicle has already insured it.